LONDON'S B

C000181215

Jack Rosenthal was born in Manchester in 1931, though he now finds this hard to believe (the date, not the place). He read English at Sheffield University and Russian (just) as a National Serviceman in the Royal Navy. He wrote his autobiography at the age of nine (a slim volume).

He began writing for television in 1961 with Episode 30 of *Coronation Street*, and went on to write over 150 further episodes, as well as scores more for many drama and comedy series, including *That Was the Week that Was*.

He created three comedy series of his own: *The Dustbinmen, The Lovers* (Writers' Guild Best Comedy Series Award, 1971) and *Sadie, It's Cold Outside*.

He has written some 27 TV films and plays, achieving a unique treble in winning three British Academy Best Play Awards in three successive years. His works include: *Another Sunday & Sweet F.A.* (TV Critics' Circle Best Play Award, 1972); *The Evacuees* (British Academy Best Play Award, Broadcasting Press Guild Best Play Award, International Emmy Award, 1975; *Bar Mitzvah Boy* (British Academy Best Play Award, Broadcasting Press Guild Best Play Award, 1976); *Ready When You Are, Mr McGill.* (British Academy Best Play Nomination, 1976); *Spend, Spend, Spend* (British Academy Best Play Award and Italia Prize Nomination, 1977); *The Knowledge* (British Academy Best Play Nomination and Italia Prize Nomination, 1979), *P'Tang, Yang, Kipperbang* (British Academy Best Play Nomination, 1982); *Day to Remember* (San Francisco Film Festival Special Jury Award, 1987) and *London's Burning* (British Academy Best Play Nomination, 1987).

He is a winner of both the British Academy Writer's Award and the Royal Television Society Writer's Award.

His feature films include *The Chain, Lucky Star* (Cannes Award and Canadian Academy Best Screenplay Award) and *Yentl*, co-written with Barbra Streisand.

His stage plays include *Dear Anyone* (Cambridge Theatre) and *Smash!* (Richmond Theatre).

He lives in London with his wife, actress Maureen Lipman, their daughter Amy, son Adam and cat Pushkin (sometimes also known as The Youthful Eel).

LONDON'S BURNING

The screenplay of the original film
of *London's Burning*

Jack Rosenthal

 Robson Books

First published in Great Britain in 1989 by Robson Books Ltd,
Bolsover House, 5–6 Clipstone Street, London W1P 7EB

British Library Cataloguing in Publication Data

Rosenthal, Jack, *1931*—
London's Burning.
I. Title
822'.914

ISBN 0 86051 573 7

Photoset and printed in Great Britain by
Redwood Burn Limited, Trowbridge, Wiltshire

Principal characters, in order of appearance, in London Weekend Television's production of *London's Burning*

Ethnic	Gary McDonald
Vaseline	Mark Arden
Bayleaf	James Hazeldine
Tate	James Marcus
Hallam	Sean Blowers
Malcolm	Rupert Baker
Sicknote	Richard Walsh
Charisma	Gerard Horan
Rambo	Jerome Flynn
Josie	Katharine Rogers
Executive producers	Linda Agran
	Nick Elliott
Producer	Paul Knight
Director	Les Blair

London's Burning was first transmitted on 7 December 1986

Ethnic

Vaseline

Bayleaf

Tate

Hallam

Malcolm

Sicknote

Charisma

Rambo

Josie

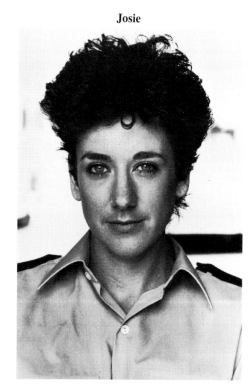

INTRODUCTION

London's Burning was a long time in the kindling. It was finally written in 1985, but the initial spark happened seven years earlier, which was when I first met a London fireman by the name of Les Murphy.

Up till then, and I imagine in common with the rest of the public who'd never had their fingers burnt dialling 999, my attitude to firemen seemed to have been coloured by a sort of cartoon mythology which pigeon-holed them with ancient Enid Blyton postmen on bikes and long-gone village coppers on their beat.

You saw a fire-engine clanging down the High Street – and your immediate reaction was to smile.

I'm not sure why this was. Maybe it was because – just as civil servants are traditionally supposed to drink tea all day – firemen are supposed to slide down poles. Maybe it was because they rescued moggies from trees. Or maybe there was an even simpler reason: that they really did grow up to become what we only *said* we would . . .

Motorists, of course, didn't smile. With a deafening, red-blurred juggernaut engulfing their driving mirrors, they just lunged on to the pavement, slammed on their brakes and swore.

Those whose homes .he firemen were hurtling to, of course, neither smiled nor swore. To them, firemen were heroes.

By now, though, times have changed, and we've changed with them. The cartoon mythology has gone up in flames. We watch almost nightly telecasts of horror – from terrorists' carnage to such obscenities as the furnace of the Bradford City football ground.

Firemen, we all now know, *are* heroes.

*

Back in 1978, we had a Swiss au pair girl, Ruth. Her boyfriend was Fireman Les Murphy. When they got married they lived with us for a year, and ever since Les has called in to see us

9

about once a week. It was listening to the stories that Les told me – or, just as often, wanting to hear the ones he was too exhausted or modest or upset to tell – that gave me the itch to write this film. With each story I realized more and more that the Fire Brigade was not only a whole world of its own, but a uniquely dramatic one of clashing opposites.

Firefighters are unique in that – unlike soldiers or policemen to whom danger and possible death are a virtual *raison d'être* – they are civilians. They don't face flick-knives, guns or bombs. They live at home with their families and go off to work like the rest of us. We catch lifts up to offices or clock on in factories and the firemen cross the threshold into the fire station. And there the similarity stops dead. Across the threshold is no man's land. Beyond *that* could be the nightmare of the fire at King's Cross. At any moment in the next eight hours they might be fighting for people's lives in a literal hell of pitch-black smoke and searing infernos. Mostly they win, sometimes they lose. If they lose, they're the ones who scrape up the ashes in the ashes of buildings or cars or trains. Then they go home like the rest of us, cursing the traffic jams and wandering what's on telly tonight. Back to the unreality of what the rest of us take to be reality. Their day's work's behind them and forgotten. Or, more truthfully, half-forgotten. There's one exception: the memory of a child's corpse *never* goes away.

Well, that's *half* of what a firefighter's day (or night) might be like. In spite of it – or, no doubt, because of it, the other half is its opposite. In the intervals between alarm bells ringing (apart from drill that has to be done, equipment to be maintained and the station to be kept clean) there are 'wheezes' to be played.

If life-and-death struggles are the ultimate reality, wheezes are as surreal as firemen sliding *up* a pole. Wheezes are painstakingly elaborate, often ingenious, often cruel practical jokes. Many of them the rest of us grew out of round about the time we grew out of wanting to be firemen. And they're probably what keeps firefighters sane – or mad enough to do the job they do.

This double life of extremes – tragedy and farce, heroism and silliness – breeds more opposites: a compassion for the victims of fires and no sympathy whatever for each other. A firefighter, wolfing his statutory (and beloved) cheese-and-onion rolls at the Mess table, wouldn't dream of saying he had a headache or he couldn't pay his mortgage or his wife was leaving him. At best, he'd get half a dozen Coke cans hurled straight at his headache, he'd be told to go and live in a tent and his mates would ask for his wife's new phone number. If he was fool enough to show that any of these upset him even more, they'd keep it up for anything between six months and a lifetime.

The uniqueness of their world has naturally produced an indigenous wit and language among firemen. The nearest to it, I suppose, is that of sailors (the Fire Brigade is closely related to the Royal Navy in several ways). But there's a speed of repartee, an (often brutal) incisiveness and invention among firefighters that I rarely witnessed in my two years' National Service in the Royal Navy – but witnessed almost non-stop in my two days at a fire station.

*

Over the years, in weekly instalments, Les Murphy told me stories of the tragedies, the wheezes, the Mess table dramas of his daily life. There was obviously enough 'insider' factual material for a documentary. Or maybe ten. There was enough tragedy for a series of mini-series or enough fun for a long-running comedy show. But I wanted to concentrate all three elements in one TV film; to dramatize the in-built opposites – and to personify even more conflicting opposites that involved the rest of us much as they did firemen. I came up with two.

The first was to introduce a female firefighter into this stridently, jealously-macho world. A woman who, like all women, would be all things to all men. In this case, initially a resented intruder, scorned as a would-be equal, but gradually accepted as one-of-the-boys as well as a girl, and finally welcomed as a pal, a professional firefighter and herself.

The second arose from the tragic night of the Broadwater Farm riot in Tottenham in October 1985. For a long time before the riot itself, Broadwater Farm had been becoming a no-go area for most outsiders, a barbed-wire tightrope for most of its residents and a minefield for firemen. Often the Brigade would be lured inside by hoax 999 calls. Once there they'd be bombarded with paving-stones dropped from the balconies. To the small core of hard men of the ghetto, a fireman's uniform represented the same badge of Authority as a policeman's – and provoked the same hatred. P.C. Blakelock who was grotesquely murdered at the riot was in the act of protecting firemen when he was ambushed.

It was after seeing newscasts of the riot that I seriously began to think of a dramatic framework for Les's stories and of a fictional centre for the film which would make the fact all the more true. I went out on 'shouts' with the men from Hornsey Fire Station and lived with them for two days and a night, I rode with the men from the Fire Brigade's elite team at Shaftesbury Avenue (which covers the 'fire-a-minute' square mile of Soho); I listened to officers from Brigade HQ, black firefighters, women firefighters, Rastafarians, inhabitants of Broadwater Farm – and, gobsmacked, observed the antics of my fellow-members of the public at each 'incident'.

The fictional centre of the film is Ethnic – a character who is (as many are) both black and a member of the London Fire Brigade; who – at at one and the same time – feels loyalty both to his ghetto community and to his fellow-firefighters; and who becomes the pivot of extremes and colliding opposites. That's why 'Ethnic' was born – and why, at the end of the film, he dies.

En route, his character gave me the chance to try and explore the deprivation and bitterness of ghetto-life and the victims of racism . . . and to show how inevitably bitterness flares into petty street violence, and that violence into cold-blooded, hot-blooded, meaningless murder. To try and understand from both points of view. And to offer the viewers of *London's Burning*, if not an understanding, then, at least, the fact that there is something we have to understand and do something about. Or live (or die) to regret it.

1. A SMALL BLACK STREET KID
*Seated on the ground, playing aimlessly and emptily
with an old, battered Coke can and half a brick.*
*He – and the shot – should look as reminiscent as is
realistically possible of the Oxfam advertisement of a
black kid in Africa, playing with a pebble on the
parched earth.*
*Our boy is older, better-fed and better (albeit thread-
barely) clothed.*
*But they should evoke the same mood of resigned
hopelessness.*
PULL BACK
*to see our boy is seated, not in Ethiopia, but in a
bleak, derelict street in the middle of a dilapidated
concrete ghetto in inner London. In 1986.*
*Behind him is a Community Hall. On the door is an
amateurishly designed poster, reading: 'Afternoon Jam
Down – Admission FREE – Soul Food all-in!'*
*Near by is an older black boy (the Aerosol Kid)
spraying graffiti on the wall.*
*Throughout the above, we hear the music of a band
coming from the Hall.*

2. INT. COMMUNITY HALL. DAY
*The audience is sparse and composed entirely of
middle-aged or elderly female Blacks. They're all
having a ball, clapping or stamping ill-shod feet to the
music of four young men, dressed as smoothly as they
can afford. These are Claude, Maxwell, Lloyd and
Ethnic – known as the Ghetto Blasters. They're not
enjoying their music as much as the audience (a
resignedly dated number like 'The Banana Boat Song')
and they're bored out of their Michael Jackson*

13

haircuts. At the back of the hall is a trestle table with tea urn, crockery and biscuits, patties and rotis. Standing beside it is an attractive black girl – Charlene. She grins at Ethnic – and gives him a thumbs-up sign. He grins back.

3. EXT. COMMUNITY HALL. DAY
The Aerosol Kid lowers his spray for a moment, in disgust at the music. He turns to the Street Kid.
AEROSOL KID: You ever hear sounds like that in your life? Blouse n' skirts, them folks must be *well* old.
STREET KID (*deadpan*): Don't knock it, man. They get free biscuits.
His pal resumes his paint-spraying.
DISSOLVE TO

4. THE STROKES OF A PAINT BRUSH
wielded by a man at the top of a ladder outside a salubrious house in, say, Hampstead Garden Suburb. The man is about 35 years old, dressed in decorator's once-white overalls. This is Bayleaf. He's painting the drainpipes and windowsills.
AT THE FRONT DOOR
The lady of the house pops her head out. This is Mrs Webb. She looks up at Bayleaf.
MRS WEBB: Are you up in the air?
BAYLEAF (*calling down*): Either that or your house is shrinking, Mrs Webb . . .
MRS WEBB: Only I think I'm getting hysterical again.
BAYLEAF (*glances at his watch*): Yeah, I think you're about due . . . nearly five o'clock.
He resignedly gathers his paints and brushes and starts to descend.

5. INT. THE WEBBS' GARAGE. DAY
Bayleaf is stacking away his paints and turpentined brushes on to wall-shelves.

14

*Mrs Webb stands beside him agonizing over a
decorator's colour-chart.*

MRS WEBB: I just don't know if it's too mushroomy.

BAYLEAF: It has to dry out, that's only the
undercoat . . .

MRS WEBB: But for the *topcoat* . . .

BAYLEAF: You wanted Sudden Sunset for the topcoat!
You said it had a touch of the cerise you fancied
in the whatsit . . . Hawaian Twilight Pink. I wish
they had proper names – I keep having to slap my
wrist . . .

MRS WEBB: I thought we changed the Sudden Sunset
to Golden Aubergine?

BAYLEAF: No, dear. Golden Aubergine to the Sudden
Sunset.

*He starts taking his overalls off. Underneath are
revealed a petrel-blue shirt and dark blue trousers.*

MRS WEBB: I *am* a pain, aren't I?

BAYLEAF: We'll sort it all out next Wednesday.

MRS WEBB: I do mess you about.

BAYLEAF: Imagine how the *paint* feels.

6. EXT. THE REAR GARDEN OF MRS GRANT'S LARGE
HOUSE. DAY

*A man of about 30 is raking garden refuse into a big
fitfully burning mound, next to an ornate garden shed.
He's bare-chested and wearing old, torn trousers and
gumboots. His name is Vaseline.*

*He then makes his way to the back door of the
house. He starts kicking the soil off his gumboots
against the wall, while knocking at the door.*

*As he does so, the middle-aged lady of the house (Mrs
Grant) opens her kitchen window. Vaseline sees her.*

MRS GRANT: It's not time for off, is it? (*searches
through her purse*) You'll do the south-facing wall
Wednesday week, then?

VASELINE: Thursday.

She stops. Looks at him, anxiously.

15

MRS GRANT: I thought *Wednesday's* your next free
day . . .
VASELINE: I'm in the Divorce Court, Wednesday.
MRS GRANT: I thought that was *Thursday?*
VASELINE: Nah, Thursday I'm getting married.
MRS GRANT: (*bleak smile*) Oh. Got it wrong.
(*recovering*) And where are you going for your
honeymoon?
VASELINE: Bleeding Divorce Court again, the way it's
going . . .
Mrs Grant smiles, uncertainly, and starts counting
notes and pound coins from her purse.
MRS GRANT: Fifteen, isn't it, and you prefer cash . . .
VASELINE: Ta.
MRS GRANT: Five, ten, and one, two, three, four . . .
I'll have to owe you one . . .
VASELINE: Oh. Right.
Mrs Grant closes the kitchen window. Vaseline
starts back towards the shed.
VASELINE: (*to himself, muttering angrily*) I won't owe
you one, darling. Bloody *give* you one, yes.
He goes into the shed.

7. INT. COMMUNITY HALL. DAY
The audience is applauding the end of the concert. The
four young men take a relieved bow. A plump Mistress
of Ceremonies waddles to the centre stage. This is Rose.
ROSE: Well, thank you, Brothers. Ladies and
Gentlemen, well, Ladies . . . (*she gestures towards*
the young men) The Ghetto Blasters!
Another round of applause and another bow.
And we'd like to thank them for they take time
off from all that Soul and Reggae stuff, and give
us such a good time.
Corroborative shouts from the audience (Yeah!
Yeah!).

16

And now, if everyone'll move their chairs over to the table, we all have a little tea-party while Sister Lilah reads our tea leaves.

As the audience complies, the Ghetto Blasters start packing their instruments away.

ETHNIC: Rehearsal next Wednesday, Brothers?

LLOYD: Right.

ETHNIC: See you then.

He goes off, with his packed guitar, towards the refreshment stand, where Charlene and a middle-aged woman are organizing the refreshments. The woman is Beatrice, Ethnic's mother.

ETHNIC: You take my strings back to our yard for me, Ma?

BEATRICE: Sure.

She takes the guitar and hands him a carrier bag. He and Charlene snatch a quick kiss. Charlene turns quickly to see if Beatrice has noticed. She has.

BEATRICE: That's O.K., Charlene. That's allowed.

Charlene grins and hands Ethnic one of the cakes from the stand. Beatrice slaps Ethnic's wrist.

That *ain't*!

ETHNIC: (*to Charlene*) See you tomorrow, babe.

(*to Beatrice*) See you tomorrow, Ma.

He exits, with the carrier bag, munching the cake.

8. EXT. COMMUNITY HALL. DAY

The two kids are still there, as before. Ethnic comes out of the door, carrying his carrier-bag.

The Street Kid calls out to him.

STREET KID: Hey, man, we been listening to you.

ETHNIC: (*pleased*) That right?

STREET KID: Right. And you know what I want to be when I grow up?

ETHNIC: (*still walking away*) What?

STREET KID: Deaf.

Ethnic picks up a piece of rubble and slings it at

him. The Kid slings it back. Ethnic goes on his way.

9. INT. CASH 'N CARRY STORE. DAY
Bayleaf is at the check-out till, re-loading groceries into a box.

The young, female Cashier takes an economy pack of bacon from the counter, ready to punch out the price on the till.

CASHIER: And 28 packets of streaky bacon, right?

BAYLEAF: Right.

CASHIER: Not like you getting streaky. I thought your lot were Best Back merchants?

BAYLEAF: If they ever get round to putting their hands in their pockets, they could have Best Back caviare. Till then, streaky or nothing.

CASHIER: You love 'em deep down, don't you?

BAYLEAF: Yeah, well . . . they grow on you. Like a bunch of veruccas.

She rings up the price on the till.

10. EXT. MRS GRANT'S BACK GARDEN. DAY
Vaseline emerges from the garden shed, now wearing the same petrel-blue shirt and dark trousers that Bayleaf is wearing. He's stuffing his old gardening pants and gumboots into an ex-army satchel.

As he starts for the side (exit) door of the house, Mrs Grant appears at her back door.

MRS GRANT: *(calling)* I say!

Vaseline stops in his tracks.

MRS GRANT: Rubbish!

VASELINE: Who is?

She points to the mound of garden rubbish, still smouldering. Vaseline turns.

VASELINE: Oh. Right.

He returns to the mound, and stamps on it till the wisps of smoke die away. He waits for Mrs Grant to go back in again, then promptly straightens up, and clears off.

11. EXT. GHETTO ESTATE. DAY
It's populated with youths lounging around, chatting, whistling at passing girls, trying to fix unfixable old bangers; gossiping women; elderly people, sitting in silence at their doorsteps; kids playing. The majority is black – but not all.

An air of aimlessness, uselessness.

Ethnic threads his way through them, with his carrier bag. He sees two young Rastafarians and a white boy (Whitey) leaning against a wall ahead of him. They see him.

There's the slightest hint of hesitation in Ethnic's walk. He recovers and continues towards them. They

*stare at him the whole time. An increasing feeling of
tension and menace. As he passes them –*

1ST RASTA: So's wha you are carry in dat bag dey
den, Brudder?

Ethnic's hand grips his carrier-bag harder.

ETHNIC: Nothin'.

2ND RASTA: It look a heap too ram-out for nothin'.

He snatches the bag from Ethnic and looks inside.

ETHNIC: Clothes for work.

*2nd Rasta pulls out of the bag a petrel-blue shirt
and dark blue trousers.*

1ST RASTA: What work's dat, mister?

ETHNIC: (*a beat*) Sweepin up. Part-time.

1ST RASTA: Jah Rasta-fari?

ETHNIC: Right.

2ND RASTA: Let's hear it, Brudder.

ETHNIC: True to Jah.

*They stuff the clothes back in the bag and thrust it
back at him.*

1ST RASTA: Just chilling out, man.

ETHNIC: That's cool.

He walks on. When he is some feet away . . .

2ND RASTA: Don't mess with I and I, right?

*Ethnic turns, nods agreement, then continues on
his way.*

12. EXT. CORNER OF ESTATE. DAY

*Ethnic rounds the corner, clutching his carrier-bag.
Now ahead of him he sees two policemen patrolling the
street. Again, his step falters for a moment.*

*Again a feeling of tension, as the two policemen
watch him approach, their eyes sharpening in
suspicion.*

As he's about to pass them . . .

1ST P.C: In a hurry, Sambo?

ETHNIC: My name ain't Sambo. Like yours ain't
Honky.

1ST P.C: You calling me Honky?

ETHNIC: No. That's what I *wasn't* calling you . . .

2ND P.C: (*nodding towards carrier-bag*) What you
got, then? Heroin or ganja?

ETHNIC: Clothes for work.

1ST P.C: What work's that, then, Sambo?

*He grabs the bag and pulls out the shirt and
trousers. The two P.C.s look at each other, then at
him. Now they're smiling at him amicably. Even
with respect. The 1ST P.C. pushes the clothes back
inside the bag; the 2ND P.C. pats Ethnic on the
head.*

2ND P.C: Sorry about that, mate. Just doing our job.
Good lad.

Ethnic sighs and walks on.

13. INT. UNSAVOURY VIDEO SHOP. DAY

The equally unsavoury Proprietor is behind the

counter, checking two video cassettes which BAYLEAF *is handing over to him.*

PROPRIETOR: Right, so that's two returned ... any idea what you want to take?

BAYLEAF: Anything new in?

The Proprietor glances through his counter display.

PROPRIETOR: *Rampant Shopgirls.*

BAYLEAF: They've seen that. Pirate copy ...

PROPRIETOR: Um ... *Susan Rides the Rangers* ...

BAYLEAF: That'll do. They've got *Panorama* tonight anyway ...

14. INT. FIRE STATION APPLIANCE ROOM. DAY

It's 6 p.m. A new duty-watch is mustered in a straight line: seven men wearing yellow helmets, black fire-tunic, belt, yellow leggings and boots.

They include Bayleaf, Vaseline and Ethnic. The others are Rambo, Malcolm, Charisma and Sick Note. (Malcolm is ex-public school. Rambo ceaselessly flexes his muscles. Charisma is almost unnoticeable. Sick Note is nursing a tooth-ache).

Station Officer Tate and Sub-Officer Hallam walk towards them, past the two fire-engines (known hereafter as 'machines' or 'pumps' or 'appliances').

They stop in front of the men.

TATE: (*to Hallam*) Call the roll.

HALLAM: Blue Watch – attention! (*The men stand to attention – with varying degrees of smartness.*) Answer your names. (*He lists the names from his clipboard*) Leading Fireman Cross.

MALCOLM: Yes, sir.

HALLAM: Fireman Wilson.

BAYLEAF: Sir.

HALLAM: Fireman Cartwright.

VASELINE: Sir.

HALLAM: Fireman Lewis.

22

ETHNIC: Yes, sir.

HALLAM: Fireman Quigley? (*No answer from Sick Note.*) Fireman Quigley!? (*Sick Note holds his jaw as though in great pain.*) Sick Note I know you're there. Would you do me the honour of answering your name?

SICK NOTE: I've got a tooth-ache, sir. I can't talk.

HALLAM: Fireman Quigley.

SICK NOTE: Here, sir.

HALLAM: Fireman Appleby.

CHARISMA: Sir.

HALLAM: Fireman Baines.

RAMBO: Sir.

HALLAM: Blue Watch, Stand at ease! (*They do so.*) Riders for appliances are as follows (*reads from clipboard*) – On the pump-ladder, myself, Fireman Appleby driving, plus Leading Fireman

Cross and Fireman Baines. On the pump; Station
Officer Tate, Fireman Wilson driving, plus
Fireman Lewis and Fireman Cartwright.
Watchroom – Fireman Quigley. Detached Duty –
Fireman Murphy; Fireman Shaw acting up;
Fireman Underwood, long-term sick.

RAMBO: (*to whoever's next to him*) The replacement
en't turned up.

HALLAM: Chemical Protection Suits – Cartwright and
Lewis, Baines and Cross. Blue Watch – atten . . .

RAMBO: 'Scuse me, sir. I thought we was getting a
replacement for Liver Salts.
Tate immediately looks a little uncomfortable.
Hallam shoots him a glance. As though they share
a guilty secret. Tate nods for Hallam to continue.
He does so.

HALLAM: Blue Watch – atten . . .

RAMBO: We're one short without Liver Salts . . .

TATE: (*testily*) We know that, son. One of the pre-
requisites of my job is being able to count up to
ten. That, and being cooped up with the
criminally insane all night without eating the
wallpaper.

HALLAM: (*after another glance at Tate*) Fireman
Andrews' replacement arrives from J Division
suppertime, alright?

TATE: Happy now?

HALLAM: Blue Watch – attention! For duty, fall out!

TATE: Give it an hour – then Make and Mend.
The men move to the two machines and begin
checking the equipment. As they do so . . .

RAMBO: (*to the world at large*) I was only pointing it
out . . .

BAYLEAF: Well, put it back. You get six months for
that.

ETHNIC: Well, you ought to know.

RAMBO: (*watching the departing TATE*) He's hiding

24

something. I can tell. Twitching and scratching.
It's what they call Body Language.
MALCOLM: Oh, yes?
RAMBO: They did a book on it. *The Naked Monkey.*
By Richard Attenborough.
MALCOLM: (*a beat*) Um ... I don't think you've got
that absolutely spot on, actually.
BAYLEAF: (*to Malcolm*) Don't argue with him. Don't
even listen. He'll start telling you what bleedin'
chapter.
RAMBO: Chapter Four. About half-way down.

15. EXT. STATION YARD. DAY
*The Watch is in the middle of Fire Drill; scaling the
ladder up to the tower and training their hose into a
corner of the yard. Tate and Hallam stand to one side,
supervising – and occasionally dodging the jet. Both of
them still edgy and fidgety.*
TATE: You know what they're like. They'll go bleedin'
spare. If I'd told them at Roll Call, they'd have
shinned over the wall, never to be seen again.
(*sighs*) Finished up in some tattoo parlour in
Montevideo. We'd have had to call Interpol.
HALLAM: Well, they'll see for themselves in a minute.
TATE: God help us.
HALLAM: Have you ever worked with one before?
TATE: In my day we joined the Brigade to get away
from them. Like the Foreign Legion but handier
for White Hart Lane.
HALLAM: I'm impressed.

16. EXT. STREET OUTSIDE FIRE STATION. EVENING
*A small queue stands at the bus-stop. Near the feet of
the last man in the queue is a five-pound note. He
glances at the others to see if they've noticed it. Satisfied
that they haven't, he bends down as nonchalantly as
possible to pick it up.*
Just as his fingers are closing over it, it flutters away

from him and settles down at the feet of a woman in the queue.

As the man goes for it, the woman notices it and bends down to pick it up. It promptly flutters away again. A youth tries to grab it. It dances away from him, and as they all try to catch it fluttering in mid-air, it suddenly leaps away and starts floating upwards towards the window of the Mess in the Fire Station.

The queue watches.

From the P.O.V. of the window, we see the bus queue watch, open-mouthed, as the fiver dances towards us.

17. INT. FIRE STATION MESS/KITCHEN. CONTINUOUS
EVENING
Amid whoops of schoolboy glee from Malcolm, he and

*Rambo are at the window, hauling in a line to which
the five-pound note is attached.*
*The Mess is furnished with a long, rectangular table
with a dozen chairs around it. A cat is asleep on it.
There are two phones – one for the Brigade, the other
public.*
CUT TO THE KITCHEN
*which is adjoining, and visible through a wall-sized
serving hatch.*
*Bayleaf (who is Mess manager) is stacking away his
Cash 'n Carry groceries into freezer, fridge and larder.
On the massive stove, a huge dixie is bubbling away.
From time to time, Bayleaf takes time off from his
stacking away to taste the contents of the dixie from a
long wooden spoon.*
CUT TO THE MESS
Vaseline calls to Bayleaf.
VASELINE: What is it tonight? Dungburgers?
BAYLEAF: *Camel* dungburgers.
RAMBO: Again.
ETHNIC: (*to Bayleaf*) I'm getting a taste for 'em.
  Bloody *had* to since you became Mess
  manager . . .
MALCOLM: What's on the à la carte?
  *Malcolm titters at his witticism. The others all
  share a pained glance, muttering 'Nice one,
  Malcolm', 'Sharp, inn'e, tonight', etc.*
  Bayleaf comes to the hatch.
BAYLEAF: For the less ignorant among you – get the
  cat off the table – for the less ignorant among you
  – which probably *is* the cat – it's beef curry
  and . . .
  *A great, wailing moan of disappointed disgust
  from all of them.*
  . . . and rice and . . . (*Another incredulous moan*)
  . . . and tinned apricots and custard for afters.

27

In the beef curry is red peppers, green peppers, a touch of garlic. . .

RAMBO: I'm going to throw up.

VASELINE: Well, don't do it on the table. He'll –
(*meaning Ethnic*) – *eat* it.

ETHNIC: (*Nazi salute*) *Sieg Heil*, Herr Vaseline!

VASELINE: Racist.

BAYLEAF: And while we're on the subject of your guts, you're all in arrears. (*To Ethnic*) You're £8.50. (*To Vaseline*) You're £9.50, and . . .

ETHNIC: Hey, Bayleaf, if I miss out on curry, can I have double apricots?

VASELINE: You should *like* curry, being one of you lot.

ETHNIC *stares at him in grimacing disbelief.*

ETHNIC: What?

VASELINE: You heard.

ETHNIC: You're as thick as Columbus was, encha? *He* thought Jamaica was India, an' all!

VASELINE: Yeah, alright, alright. The nearest *you've* ever got to Jamaica's Fulham Broadway.

ETHNIC: Exactly. 'English', right? Thank you.

BAYLEAF: Did I hear someone say 'Thank you'?? In *here*?? Must be my earholes. Suddenly got this manky earhole.

VASELINE: Funny that, your *arse*-hole's always sounded very healthy.

The public phone abruptly rings. Bayleaf takes it.

BAYLEAF: (*into phone*) Pig sty.

18. INT. FIRE STATION WATCHROOM. EVENING
A desk, filing cabinets, teleprinter, alarm bells etc. Sick Note Quigley is at the telephone switchboard. He speaks into the mouthpiece.

SICK NOTE: That you, Bayleaf? Sick Note here. Tell Vaseline it's Marion.

He connects the call.

19. INT. KITCHEN/MESS. CONTINUOUS IN TIME
As Sc. 17.
BAYLEAF: (*covers mouthpiece*) Vaseline! It's for . . .
ETHNIC/BAYLEAF/MALCOLM/RAMBO: Yoo-hoo!
Vaseline comes to the phone, heart sinking.
Bayleaf hands it to him.
BAYLEAF: (*to Vaseline*) Marion.
VASELINE: Which Marion – wife or fiancée?
BAYLEAF: (*into phone*) 'Scuse me, Marion – are you
the ugly one or the *very* ugly one?
VASELINE *hastily grabs the phone from him.*
VASELINE: (*into phone*) Hello? (*he winces as she yells
at him*) Listen, if you . . . (*more yelling shuts him
up*) If you're just ringing to slag me off, can't you
wait till I'm . . .
*Her yelling shuts him up again. He sighs
resignedly and nods to Bayleaf to pass him a small
travelling clock on the windowsill. Bayleaf sets the
alarm, and holds it against the ear-piece of the
phone. Vaseline nods. Bayleaf presses the alarm
button.*
VASELINE: (*into phone*) Sorry, love. The bells have
gone down – there's a shout. (*Calls out to the
room in general*) Coming, sir!
*He hangs up. Bayleaf switches off the alarm and
returns the clock to the windowsill.*
BAYLEAF: Which one was it?
VASELINE: She never said.

20. INT. FIRE STATION REST ROOM. NIGHT
*Rambo and Sick Note are watching a blue video on the
TV. The room is furnished spartanly with the TV set at
one end and armchairs around the walls.*
   *Throughout the scene, their eyes never leave the TV
screen. Whenever (judiciously) possible, we CUT to the
action on the TV screen while Rambo's and Sick Note's
dialogue is heard, out of shot.*
SICK NOTE: My point is – she's such a lousy actress.

29

RAMBO: Actress? She *isn't* an actress . . .

SICK NOTE: Leave it out! Putting on the husky little
voice . . . cocking her peroxide head on one side
to show how sincere she is. It's pathetic.

RAMBO: She can't be all that bad at acting. She's
conned half the country to vote her in twice.

SICK NOTE: That's the tragedy, innit? (*beat*) Makes
you feel . . . I dunno, *used* . . . it's degrading . . .

21. INT. RECREATION ROOM. NIGHT
*The room contains a snooker table, a dart board and
an impressive 'all-in-one' piece of gymnastic
equipment. On it is a cardboard sign, reading: 'Please
Don't Disturb the Cobwebs.'*
  Charisma is playing snooker with Hallam.
  *Malcolm is playing darts by himself . . . parodying
TV darts commentators, as he does so . . . yelling 'One
hundred and forty' etc. with each throw.*
  *Charisma is trapped in a snooker. He's about to cue,
when he straightens up.*

CHARISMA: Did I tell you I've got to the semi-final at
the club?

HALLAM: I'm impressed.

CHARISMA: Yeah . . . got right through the
preliminaries . . . through the quarter final . . .

HALLAM: And now you're snookered to buggery, and
you can't get out of it.

CHARISMA: (*evasively*) Out of what?

HALLAM: (*unmoved*) Out of that.

CHARISMA: I got out of one hundred times worse at
my club.

HALLAM: I'm impressed.

CHARISMA: The black was here . . . (*he starts moving
the balls*) – the yellow was here . . .

HALLAM: (*calmly replacing them*) Charisma? Why is it
you're always the kipper's knickers at your club
and rubbish here?

CHARISMA: You talk to my mates at the club . . .

30

HALLAM: Why is it you got mates at the club and sod-all here?

CHARISMA: Listen, at my club . . .

HALLAM: Take your shot, Charisma.

The four bells sound, announcing supper. There's a yell, O.O.S., of 'Grub up!'

CHARISMA: Would you Adam and Eve it! Just as I was . . .

But Hallam is already on his way out of the room. Charisma calls after him.

I was going to play it off four cushions and . . .

Hallam has gone.

HALLAM (O.O.S.): I'm impressed.

CHARISMA: It's hard to concentrate with you shouting and bawling, Malcolm. At the club I'm used to proper tournament conditions . . . (*But Malcolm is*

already on his way out.) I was going to play it down to baulk with a bit of left hand side and screw it deep down to . . .
Malcolm has gone. Charisma stands for a moment, moves one of the balls an inch or so to one side, then leaves.

22. INT. MESS/KITCHEN. NIGHT
Bayleaf is at the stove ladling the curry and rice on to plates. Tate, Hallam, Malcolm, Vaseline, Ethnic, Rambo and Charisma are seated round the table – either already eating or collecting their plates from the counter. Rambo is still carefully watching Tate – who's more ill at ease than ever. Rambo nudges Malcolm to witness that Tate's body language is still at work.
  The rest of them are muttering about the meal. With the exception of Tate who pours half a bottle of HP Sauce all over his. Ethnic obligingly passes him two more full bottles of sauce.
TATE: You trying to tell me something, Ethnic?
ETHNIC: (*innocently*) Me, guv? No, guv. I wouldn't do a thing like that, guv.
VASELINE: Ignore him, guv. It's probably some fertility rite or something where he comes from.
ETHNIC: (*Nazi salute*) *Sieg Heil*, Mein Oberwanker!
VASELINE: Racist.
BAYLEAF: (*calling*) Sick Note!! Grub up!

23. INT. WATCHROOM. NIGHT
Sick Note is at the desk, stuffing sandwiches in his mouth from a brown paper bag. He hears Bayleaf, hastily swallows what he's eating and calls chokingly back.
SICK NOTE: Won't be a sec. Just doing my log bookings.
He stuffs another sandwich in his mouth.

32

24. INT. KITCHEN/MESS. NIGHT
As Sc. 22.
TATE: (*calling*) Are you eating down there?
SICK NOTE (O.O.S.): No, GUV.
TATE: Brigade orders, no food in the box!
SICK NOTE (O.O.S.): I'm not, guv.
TATE: I'm serious! Not even cat food!
RAMBO: Hey! Any chance of *me* having cat food,
    'stead of *this* pile of . . .
    The front-door bell rings. Tate freezes. Shoots a
    glance at Hallam. Rambo and the others look at
    them suspiciously. CUT TO:

25. INT. WATCHROOM. NIGHT
On hearing the bell, Sick Note hastily puts his
sandwiches in a drawer and peers out of the windows
into the night. He makes his way from the room.

26. INT. KITCHEN/MESS. NIGHT
As Sc. 24.
Tate gets to his feet.
TATE: I'll go.
He starts for the door. Vaseline watches him in disbelief.
VASELINE: The guvnor going to answer the door? Now *my* ears've gone manky.
Tate exits.
HALLAM: Watch it, Vaseline.
VASELINE: Well, how many time has he ever ...
HALLAM: Watch it.
VASELINE: – specially leaving his HP to go cold ...
HALLAM: Right. Name?
VASELINE: (*mock Jamaican accent*) Fireman Lewis. Known as Ethnic. Black as the ace of spades. Smells of old joss sticks.
Ethnic throws the jug of water all over him. Vaseline leaps up, drenched. He picks up his plate of curry and hurls it at Ethnic. Ethnic sways neatly to one side. The curry hits the wall..
HALLAM: I'm impressed.
Everyone continues eating, as though nothing has happened ... except Bayleaf.
BAYLEAF: (*to* VASELINE) Right. No apricots ...

27. INT. APPLIANCE ROOM. EVENING
Just as Sick Note is emerging from the watchroom to answer the front door, Tate comes striding down the corridor.
TATE: S'alright, Sick Note. It's only the replacement.
SICK NOTE: I can open the door, guv. The doctor says it's just heavy lifting that could do my shoulder in again – and the strained ligament in my foot is only ...
Tate stops in his tracks.
TATE: What strained ligament in your foot?
SICK NOTE: Didn't you know about that one?

TATE: (*Starting for the door again*) I'd need six years at Bart's to know all *your* bleeding ailments, mate. Go and have your supper. Mind your bad tooth.

*He stands at the door watching Sick Note make his way up towards the Mess. Tate opens the door to reveal that the replacement fireman is, in fact, a young fire*woman. *This is Josie Ingham. She stands in the street outside the front door, loaded down with her gear – wellies, helmet, tunic, leggings and hold-all. She wears 'undress' uniform.*

28. INT. STATION MESS/KITCHEN. EVENING
From over the shoulders of Tate and Josie as they enter, we see a shock wave runs through the faces of the men who've turned to see them come in.

Though the men's reactions are varied – and for the most part, restrained – they all express in different degrees their concern or displeasure or disbelief or dismay. Someone drops his knife and fork. Half-audible mutterings of 'Jesus . . . !' 'That's all we need . . . !' and the like.

CUT TO REVERSE ANGLE
Tate looks apprehensive and uncomfortable. Josie smiles wryly, philosophically to herself.

TATE: Um . . . er . . . Attention, Blue Watch . . . um . . . this is our new hand, replacing Fireman Andrews . . . um . . . Fire – um – *Woman* Ingham. *(to Josie)* Um . . . Josie, I believe, right?

JOSIE: Yes, sir.

TATE: Right. Um . . . now then . . . *(introducing the nearest fireman)* This is . . .
The teleprinter bell rings and a few seconds later the air is ripped apart by the clanging of alarm bells. It's a shout. Yells of 'Bollocks!'

29 INT. WATCHROOM. EVENING
On the wall, two bulbs – one red, one green – are lit up.

SICK NOTE: All the lot!

30 INT. STATION MESS/KITCHEN. EVENING
Everyone promptly crashes out of their chairs and races out of the door, barging past Tate and Josie.
Tate nods towards Josie's hold-all.

TATE: That your gear?

JOSIE: Yes, sir.

TATE: *(indicating the door)* After you, then.

JOSIE: What?
Tate realizes gentlemanly manners don't apply in the present circumstances.

TATE: Oh. Right.
He races out, followed by Josie. Then, over his shoulder –

TATE: You're with Vaseline, okay?

36

31. INT. CORRIDOR. EVENING
Some men race towards the staircase, others towards
the exposed sliding pole.

32. INT. POLE HOUSE. EVENING
– the men sliding swiftly down the pole.

33. INT. WATCHROOM, EVENING
The two bulbs on the wall are showing red and green –
the teleprinter is chattering on Sick Note's desk.
*   Hallam and the two drivers – Bayleaf and Charisma*
– are poring over the teleprinter. Tate rips the sheet
from the printer.
SICK NOTE: Viaduct Workshops. Back St James'
   Street.
   He grabs two route-cards from a file, hands one to
   Tate and one to Hallam.

37

BAYLEAF: I know where it is . . .

CHARISMA: Hang about.

He goes to a large wall map to check.

SICK NOTE: It's an abcess, I think.

TATE: What is?

SICK NOTE: (*wincing in agony*) I'm coming with you, though. I'm used to pain.

TATE: I can't leave you here. It's *verboten.*

SICK NOTE: I know – I don't want you to.

He yelps in pain and clutches his jaw. Tate sighs.

TATE: Stop where you are. We're better off without you. Don't talk to no strange men while we're gone.

BAYLEAF: And stick all the dinners back in the oven, alright?

SICK NOTE: Right.

BAYLEAF: One at a time. In case you dislocate something.

With the exception of Sick Note, they all race out to the Station Yard.

34. INT. APPLIANCE ROOM. EVENING

Bayleaf races to the driver's cabin of the machine.
Vaseline and Josie jump in the back. Ethnic is already in, changing into fire-fighting rig.
Tate runs to the passenger seat and jumps in.
Hallam hauls himself into the passenger seat of the next machine, with Charisma hurling himself into the driver's seat. Malcolm and Rambo jump into the back seat.
　　The engines roar into life.

35. INT. WATCHROOM. EVENING

Sick Note presses two buttons.

36. INT. APPLIANCE ROOM. EVENING

The automatic doors concertina open. The two machines race off into the evening.

*[N.B. The time elapsed between the alarm first
sounding and the machines driving out of the gates is
between twenty and thirty seconds.]*

37. INT. PUMP-LADDER CABIN (TRAVELLING).
EVENING
*As the machine hurtles down the street, sirens howling
and blue lamp flashing, Tate, Vaseline, Ethnic and
Josie are changing rapidly into their fire-fighting rig
(hung in front of them), while seated on their seats.
(Not easy – with the machine lurching from side to side
at top speed).*
    Bayleaf remains in undress uniform.
TATE: Which way are you going? Downton Hill?
BAYLEAF: No, Downton's too narrow with parked
    cars. I couldn't get my old man down there, let
    alone . . .
TATE: Oi!
    *Bayleaf turns, puzzled. Tate indicates a lady's
    presence in the back.*
VASELINE: You couldn't get *what* down there,
    Bayleaf?
ETHNIC: (*to Vaseline*) Evil, encha?
    Josie – still changing – pays no attention.

38. EXT. MAIN STREET. EVENING
*The two machines hurtle down the streets, lights
flashing, sirens screaming.*
    *Cars ahead pull on to the pavement hastily, out of
their way.*
    *At the traffic lights, showing red, the two machines
lurch over to the wrong side of the road – through the
lights – then swerve back to the left.*

39. EXT. ROW OF WORKSHOP/GARAGES. EVENING
*. . . in an alleyway between back-to-back houses. Two
of the ramshackle, converted workshops are burning.*

Knots of people from the neighbouring houses are standing around. The overall feeling among them is one of importance and excitement that it's happening on their street.

The two machines are parked at the corner, their blue lights spinning.

Blue Watch is briskly at work: Tate and Hallam are orchestrating the operation, talking to a note-taking policeman and members of the public. Charisma is at the controls at the rear of the pump-ladder. Rambo and Malcolm pull hose-reels and branches from the drum and start towards the blaze. Bayleaf, getting rigged in fire-fighting uniform, is speaking into the R/T, in the cab of the pump.

BAYLEAF: Code One. No problem.

Tate approaches the cab window.

TATE: Stick a hydrant in, alright?

Bayleaf gets out of the cab, goes to the locker on the pump for the hydrant key and bar. Ethnic and Vaseline are drawing lengths of hose.

Throughout all of this, Josie stands looking and feeling out of things. Whenever she tries to do anything, she's beaten to it – just as she's about to do it . . . whether activating the hydrant, drawing off the hose-reels, even when she tries to free a hose which is fouled against the wheel of a parked car.

Everything is done expertly, swiftly but unhurriedly, efficiently, like a well-drilled team. And all as though this is no time for amateurs, playing around – or women. Josie wryly gets the message.

40. THE STREET CORNER CONTINUOUS. EVENING
Two teenage girls are standing watching JOSIE *searching for something useful to do.*

IST GIRL: That one can light *my* fire any time he likes . . .

2ND GIRL: Gorgeous, en 'e? I'd love to see him wiv
 his hosepipe in his hand . . .
They dissolve into raucous giggles at the thought.

41. EXT. THE WORKSHOP/GARAGES. CONTINUOUS
EVENING
*Vaseline, Ethnic and Malcolm are almost inside the
workshops flooding it with their jets.
Tate turns to see the onlookers beginning to get too
near.*
TATE: Someone keep that lot back, will you!
 *Josie starts towards the knot of people. She's
 beaten to it by Rambo.*
RAMBO: Come on . . . back you go. Everybody. You
 never know what's in there . . . Calor gas,
 anything. Keep well back . . .
 *The crowd obeys, excitedly. Josie's about to
 wander away again, when a middle-aged man
 leans forward from the crowd and touches her
 arm. She turns.*
MAN: 'Scuse me, son. It was us that smelled the
 burning. We reported it. Well, our Gordon. 999 –
 bingo. He *usually* gets the right number when *he*
 dials.
JOSIE: Can you just move back, please? It can be very
 danger . . .
MAN'S WIFE: Gordon's our Sheila's eldest. He once
 went to Toronto, but he couldn't settle . . .
JOSIE: You as well, madam . . . well back . . .
MAN: He was dyeing his hair and I suddenly sniffed
 and went 'Hello, can you smell burning?'
MAN'S WIFE: I did, as well, didn't I? 'Can you smell
 burning?' straight off.
 *Josie starts making her way back to the
 workshops.*
MAN: (*calling after her*) Do we claim a reward or
 anything for that?

42. EXT. AT THE MACHINES. EVENING
Ethnic and Malcolm are collecting shovels. They start
back towards the workshops.

AT THE WORKSHOPS
Rambo and Hallam are clearing the smouldering debris
and junk, so that Ethnic and Malcolm can damp them
down.

43. INT. WORKSHOPS. CONTINUOUS. EVENING
Vaseline is hosing the smouldering remains of the fire.

44. EXT. WORKSHOPS. CONTINUOUS. EVENING
Josie looks around at the rest of the Watch busily
working . . . then decisively picks up one of the hose-
reels and makes her way into the workshops.

45. INT. WORKSHOPS. CONTINUOUS. EVENING
Josie makes her way past Ethnic and Malcolm, Rambo
and Hallam and is about to operate her hose. Just as
the last wisps of smoke are dying away beneath
Vaseline's jet.
He turns to her.
VASELINE: Evening. Nice of you to turn up. Where's
the fire?
Josie, deadpan, swallows her anger.

46. INT. FIRE STATION. MESS/KITCHEN. NIGHT
The table is exactly as it was left – plates of congealed
curry, cans of Pepsi, half-eaten chunks of bread.
Vaseline's wall-mounted curry is congealed in an
elongated strip down the wall.
Bayleaf enters – and stops stone dead on seeing the
table.
BAYLEAF: I'll kill him. I will. I'll bleedin' kill him.
   Ethnic, Vaseline, Malcolm, Rambo, Josie and
Charisma walk in. All (except Ethnic and Josie) groan
on seeing the table.
BAYLEAF: (*calling out*) Sick Note! Next time you're in
the doctor's don't bother with a sick note, ask for a
Death Certificate!
SICK NOTE (O.O.S.): What've I done now? With my
bad hand?
BAYLEAF: Idle sod ... (*He grabs two plates and races*
into the kitchen towards the oven, then – to the others)
Stick 'em on the hatch. I'll stick 'em in the bleedin'
oven.
   Tate enters. Sees the curry on the wall.
TATE: Get that mess off the wall, before I stick you *all*
in the bleedin' ... (*suddenly aware of Josie*) ... er ...
ruddy oven.
   Vaseline sets off to the kitchen.
VASELINE: Where's the bucket and mop?
ETHNIC: (*to Bayleaf, as he puts his plate on the hatch*)
Don't bother with mine. I'll swap it for double
apricots ...

BAYLEAF: (*at the oven*) Coming from someone who's never had a square meal in his life except from what I give you . . .
Vaseline is getting a bucket and mop from a kitchen cupboard.
VASELINE: (*to Bayleaf*) Hot dinners are *your* responsibility.
BAYLEAF: Oh, yes?
VASELINE: You're the Mess Manager.
BAYLEAF: In which case, piss off out of my kitchen.
TATE: Bayleaf, 'Kindly leave my kitchen' has precisely the same meaning as . . .
Josie is on her way into the kitchen, carrying two congealed dinners. Bayleaf stops her. Takes the plates from her.
BAYLEAF: (*tersely*) S'alright, s'alright, no panic.
Again, Josie registers her exclusion. Abruptly, the alarm sounds again. An immediate, unanimous, irritated cry of 'Bollocks!' But this time only the green light is flashing.
TATE: (*watching the green light*) Pump only!
Malcolm, Charisma and Rambo cheer and continue putting their dinners in the oven. Tate, Josie, Ethnic, Vaseline and Bayleaf race for the door.

47. EXT. MRS GRANT'S REAR GARDEN. NIGHT
The garden shed is blazing merrily. Ethnic and Vaseline are training a jet on it – and winning.
Somewhat to Ethnic's puzzlement, Vaseline seems to be going to some lengths to keep his face averted from Mr and Mrs Grant and Tate – who are standing at the back porch watching the firefighting.
TATE: I know it's not the . . . um . . . type of area . . . but you're positive it can't have been kids getting up to mischief?
MRS GRANT: No, no . . . it was definitely from the

refuse tip that the gardener ... we have this part-
time gardener ...

MR GRANT: Bit of a cowboy, really.

MRS GRANT: Yes.

*She begins to peer a little more closely at Vaseline's
averted head ... Is he? Isn't he? Can't be.*

MR GRANT: What is it, dear?

MRS GRANT: (*uncertainly*) Nothing ... You'd think I
was being silly ...

48. EXT. MRS GRANT'S STREET. NIGHT

*Bayleaf is operating the pressure gauge on the pump. A
few neighbours are watching at a distance.*

*Josie is trying to busy herself straightening the hose –
which doesn't need it.*

*A little old lady neighbour approaches her, carrying
a cup of tea.*

LITTLE OLD LADY: There was a fire at Number 37 last Christmas. In the loft conversion . . .

JOSIE: (*not interested*) Oh, yes?

LITTLE OLD LADY: They tramped wet all over her stair carpet.

JOSIE: Sorry?

LITTLE OLD LADY: The firemen. She'd put newspapers down specially, as well. Made no difference. They just went rushing up to the fire without a thought. (*hands her the tea*) There you are, Earl Grey. You feel the cold, don't you, when you're the only one standing about . . .

To Josie, it feels very much like the final insult.

JOSIE: (*shakes her head, wryly*) Thanks, anyway . . . (*She thinks for a moment, reaches a decision and walks purposefully over to Bayleaf at the pump*). Listen, Bayleaf . . .

She was wrong – it was only the penultimate insult. Bayleaf moves her slightly to one side, as though she's in the way.

BAYLEAF: Sorry, can you just . . . (*she takes a step to one side*) Ta.

She gives a sigh and starts to walk back again.

BAYLEAF: (*calling after her*) Hey! Do you want to make yourself useful? (*She turns expectantly.*) See if you can scrounge a cuppa from someone, will you?

Her face hardens.

49. INT. FIRE STATION KITCHEN/MESS. NIGHT

Tight on a mug of steaming tea.

CUT – *to see that it's Josie who's drinking it . . . seated alone at a totally cleared mess table.*

Inside the kitchen, Bayleaf is stacking the washed and dried supper dishes.

Neither he nor Josie so much as even glance at each other.

*Charisma is examining packets of food in the
freezer – much to Bayleaf's irritation.*
CHARISMA: And how much are you paying for bacon?
BAYLEAF: Out of my kitchen, please.
CHARISMA: Oh, you got streaky this time. I like
   streaky. (*Bayleaf slams the freezer door*). What's
   it costing you for streaky?
BAYLEAF: Charisma. There's the Rest Room to sit in,
   the Recreation Room to sit in, the toilets to sit in.
   Hoppit.
CHARISMA: I can get it cheaper.
BAYLEAF: Cheaper than what?
CHARISMA: Whatever you're paying.
BAYLEAF: You don't know what I'm paying.
CHARISMA: I've got a mate in my club. He can get me
   wholesale.
BAYLEAF: 97p a pound, bulk-buy. No one gets it
   cheaper.
*He pushes him out. He then stands, surveys the
cleared kitchen, and starts for the door.
As he goes, he nods, with as minimal interest as
possible, at Josie.*
BAYLEAF: Alright, then?
JOSIE: Fine.
He goes. She nurses her mug. Stay on her, then –

50. INT. REST ROOM. NIGHT
*Lounging in the armchairs are Ethnic, Malcolm and
Sick Note, watching the blue movie. Malcolm is
stretched out with his feet on a coffee table.*
SICK NOTE: What do we do if *she* comes in?
ETHNIC: Switch over to something else.
MALCOLM: We don't! We retain the status quo.
SICK NOTE: We what?
MALCOLM: We do nothing.
ETHNIC: She's a whatsit, though. A woman.
MALCOLM: So what? We don't switch off Black Magic
   commercials when *you* come in.

47

ETHNIC: Did you make that up all by yourself,
  Malcolm?
MALCOLM: (*beaming*) Good, wasn't it?
ETHNIC: Very.
  Ethnic suddenly kicks the coffee table neatly away.
  Malcolm's feet (and Malcolm) fall with a crash.
  Ethnic reaches over to the 'nutty tin' and empties
  Mars Bars, Galaxies and Milk Flakes all over him.
  Sick Note sits watching the bluey, unperturbed.

51. INT. FIRE STATION URINAL. NIGHT
Bayleaf and Hallam are having a pee.
BAYLEAF: I've got two suggestions – a) the entire
  Watch applies for a transfer, or b) we work our
  tickets, have the operation and sign on as Traffic
  Wardens.
HALLAM: I'm impressed.

52. INT. KITCHEN/MESS. NIGHT
Josie finishes her mug of tea. She gets up, goes into the
kitchen and is just about to empty the slops into the sink
before washing up the mug, when she stops. Thinks
again. Goes back into the Mess, puts the mug back on
the table and walks out.

53. INT. CORRIDOR. NIGHT
Vaseline is speaking into a wall phone – meekly and
defensively.
VASELINE: (*into phone*) I didn't, Marion! I didn't see
  any birds Sunday night . . . I was on *duty* Sunday
  night . . . (*beat*) You rang *here*? (*beat*) And
  someone told you . . . (*beat*) Who? (*beat*) Oh . . .
  Hang about, though, hang about . . . When I say
  here . . . I wasn't actually *here* . . . I had to go to Q
  Division for a special . . . (*beat*) Marion, you and
  Marion are the only birds I ever . . .
  Josie comes walking down the corridor towards
  him.

JOSIE: (*deliberately loudly as she passes*) Your flies are
    open. Again.
    Vaseline winces – tries to cover the mouthpiece.
VASELINE: (*into phone*) Who? No one . . . just one of
    the lads . . .
    We go with Josie into –

54. INT. REST ROOM. NIGHT
*Ethnic, Malcolm and Sick Note are watching the bluey
as before. Josie enters. They all turn. She sits down.
Ethnic immediately half-rises to switch the set off.
Malcolm puts out an arm to stop him. He sits down
again.*
    *They all watch in silence for a moment. Josie
deadpan; Ethnic embarrassedly; Malcolm grimly
obdurate; Sick Note agog for her to be offended.*
    After a moment, she gets up and starts to exit.
SICK NOTE: (*triumphantly*) Can't take it, eh?
JOSIE: I've seen it. Upsets me too much at the end.
MALCOLM: A little too pungent for your delicate
    nature?
JOSIE: No. The girls all gang up on him and cut his
    goolies off. I never could bear to see a grown man
    cry. Ciao.
    Ethnic grins. She exits.

55. INT. TATE'S OFFICE. NIGHT
*Tate is seated on his bunk in his underclothes. (His
clothes are immediately at hand for instant diving into).
On his bedside table is a half-completed matchstick
model of Alexandra Palace, together with photographs
identifying it. He's working on it from his bed.
There's a knock at the door.*
TATE: Come in. (*then suddenly wary*) Hang on, hang
    on! Who is it?
RAMBO: (O.O.S.) Rambo.
TATE: Come in. (*Rambo enters, looking a little
    perturbed.*) Well?

49

RAMBO: I was thinking of turning in, guv.

TATE: And?

RAMBO: Well, it's awkward, innit?

TATE: What do you want – a lullaby?

RAMBO: It's *her*, innit?

TATE: Is she in bed yet?

RAMBO: No.

TATE: You're all right, then. It's when *she* turns in,
two of you have to be present. So she's not
trapped on her tod with one of you animals. If
you want to turn in, the rule doesn't apply.

RAMBO: What if she turns in next, though? *I'll* be
trapped on my tod with *her*. What do I do?

TATE: You'll either have to cross your legs or fake an
orgasm.
Rambo sighs worriedly. He looks at Tate's model.

RAMBO: Did you know Alexandra Palace burns down
every hundred years?

TATE: It's only been there 120 . . .

RAMBO: That was where they had the Great
Exhibition, 1751.

TATE: No. *Crystal* Palace. *1851*.

RAMBO: The land's got a curse on it . . .

TATE: So's my office. Piss off. (RAMBO *sighs again,
then starts for the door, then stops again.*) Now
what?

RAMBO: I always kip starkers.

TATE: S'alright. She *looks* as though she could do with
a good laugh.
*Rambo goes, unhappily. Tate resumes his model-
making.*

56. EXT. FIRE STATION. NIGHT
*All the lights go out, except the secondary lighting on
corridors, the pole-room and the Watchroom. We see
Sick note at the Watchroom window, drawing the
curtains.*

57. INT. WATCHROOM. NIGHT
Sick Note makes his way from the window to his fold-away bed near the teleprinter. He covers himself in blankets and settles down to try and sleep.

58. INT. TATE'S OFFICE. NIGHT
Tate carefully puts his model to rest on the bedside table, settles down in his bunk and switches off the main light.

59. INT. FIRE STATION DORMITORY. NIGHT
It's in half-darkness, lit only by the corridor light outside.
Bayleaf, Ethnic, Vaseline, Malcolm, Rambo, Charisma and Josie are all in their beds.
Intercut from one face to another – all of them awake, with their own thoughts. A silence. Then . . .
JOSIE: *(sighs, resignedly)* Okay. Here we go. One – I'm not a dyke. Two – I'm not a women's libber. Three – I'm not a nymphomaniac. Four – I'm not an alien from Outer Space. *(Beat. The men risk tiny glances at each other.)* I'm in the job because I like it. I'm not clever enough to be a nurse or a secretary. But two days and two nights a week, I'm bloody good at fighting fires. The rest of the time I do the stuff other women do. My Dad was a fireman, my brother-in-law's a fireman in Leicester. I've been married for five months. I've been in the Brigade for just over a year. I've been to hundreds of shouts. *(The men soberly, chastened, avoid each other's eyes.)* So you can all behave exactly as normal – either on shouts, or in the station or in your pits. *(beat)* There's only one difference between you and me – and that's what you're no doubt holding in your hands under your blanket. So it's only a *little* difference, innit? *(beat)* And sod all to do with putting out fires. Unless you piss on them. Goodnight.

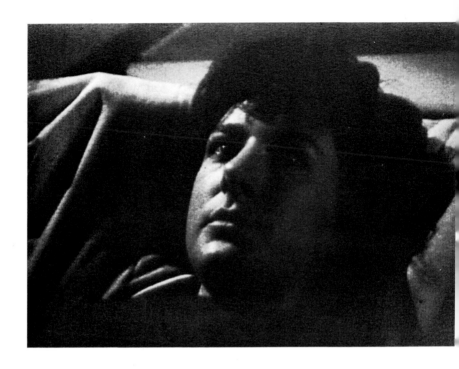

(*There's a silence ... then Ethnic starts to clap,*
appreciatively.)

RAMBO: Who's that?

VASELINE: Must be Ethnic. He's the only one whose
hands you can't see in the dark.

(*Someone farts.*)

MALCOLM: Who was that?

ETHNIC: Probably Vaseline. Saying his prayers.

VASELINE: Say that again, Dairy Box!

BAYLEAF: Alright, alright! Everyone get their heads
down, alright?

Josie lies, eyes open, staring at the ceiling. She
seems close to tears. But they're only tears of
frustration. Finally, she turns on her side and closes her
eyes.

Intercut between the different men, all beginning to
settle down to sleep.

Abruptly, the alarms jangle ear-splittingly into life.
Everyone leaps out of bed, in their underpants and
socks. (In Josie's case – bra and panties.)
They all start flinging themselves into their clothes.
DISSOLVE TO:

60. EXT. A STREET OF WORKING-CLASS HOUSES. DAY
An incongruously expensive car motors down the ill-
kempt street and stops outside a second-hand furniture
shop. Above the window a badly painted sign reads:
'Hi-Class 2nd. Hand Furniture, TV's etc. You Name
It.'
   The shop window and street frontage are littered with
dilapidated household goods, broken mangles and
junk. A white woman gets out of the car, opens the
boot and takes from it a cushioned chair.

61. INT. FURNITURE SHOP. CONTINUOUS. DAY
The (white) proprietor, stubble-chinned, dishevelled, is
stripping a pine wash-stand.
   The woman lugs in the chair and plonks it on the
floor. The proprietor looks up and nods. She nods
back and goes.
   The proprietor dries his hands on his shirt, takes the
cushion from the chair and rips it open.
   He pulls out of it several parcels wrapped in silver
foil.
PROPRIETOR: (*calling*) Max!
   A black version of the proprietor appears from the
   workroom at the back, carrying a blow-torch. The
   proprietor indicates the parcels.
MAX: Okay.

62. EXT. BLACK GHETTO. DAY
The same air of bleak, hopeless futility as before. The
young men are still fiddling with an old banger, even
more listlessly. Kids play, people pass each other with
half-hearted greetings. A rusting, clapped-out van

*comes clanking and squealing into the estate. On its
side are the words: 'Hi-Class 2nd. Hand Furniture,
TV's etc. You Name It.'*

*It stops outside one of the blocks of flats. Max gets
out, opens the rear doors and hauls out an ancient
black and white TV set.*

63. EXT. FLATS (GHETTO). DAY
*The door opens and a man (Pusher) appears at the
door. Reverse angle to see that Max is on his doorstep
with the TV set.*
MAX: One telly. Black and white.
PUSHER: I catch de beat.
    *He takes the TV set from him, lugs it in, and kicks
    the door closed.*
    ANGLE ON
    four men who are sitting in the room, waiting.

54

They watch Pusher rest the TV set in the middle of the floor.

PUSHER: Alright, Eidren. Time for 'Gardener's World'.

He rips open the back of the TV set and takes out four silver-foiled blocks of compressed marijuana. He distributes them among the men.

PUSHER: Hundred an ounce, okay?

The men nod and grunt agreement.

64. EXT. SUBURBAN SHOPPING STREET. DAY

CHARISMA – *very smartly dressed in civvies and wearing a carnation in his buttonhole – makes his way, with an air of restrained excitement, into a mini-market.*

65. INT. MINI-MARKET. DAY

The owner is serving a customer at the check-out. As the customer pays and leaves, we see Charisma emerge from behind a shelf of groceries, carrying a mound of slippery packets of bacon.

CHARISMA: Morning, Mrs Lane.

SHOPKEEPER: You look very smart today.

CHARISMA: Going to a wedding. Big mate of mine. Break his heart if I wasn't there.

SHOPKEEPER: You giving him bacon for a wedding present?

CHARISMA: No, no, . . . it's . . . um . . . this is for another big mate of mine. Best mate. We have a lot of laughs.

SHOPKEEPER: Expensive laugh, innit? 18, 19, 20 packets, streaky. £1.12 a pound, alright?

CHARISMA: (*shrugs*) Whatever, anything . . .

She starts punching the keys of the till. Charisma watches her with a desperate smile of hope.

And can you take the things off for me?

SHOPKEEPER: Things?

CHARISMA: The sticky labels.

SHOPKEEPER: Price tags?

CHARISMA: That's it.

66. EXT. GHETTO. DAY

A parade of shops. In stark contrast to the suburban shops, these are neglected, downtrodden, their windows boarded up.

Beatrice comes out of one of the shops, carrying a shopping bag.

She walks along, exchanging morning greetings with friends or neighbours.

As she walks, she notices a police transport vehicle parked down a side street. From it, comes a squad of policemen.

She walks on – and begins to notice more policemen in pairs. They're standing at corners, at staircases at the foot of each level, and at the staircases at the top of each level.

Beatrice and her neighbours – though still exchanging smiles and nods – watch the policemen with wary, puzzled, darting eyes.

She starts to make her way up one of the staircases.

67. INT. ETHNIC'S PARENTS' FLAT. DAY

Ethnic is in his shirt-tails, ironing a pair of trousers on the table. His father, Eldridge, is on his hands and knees trying to fix the heating boiler in a wall-cupboard, spanners scattered around the floor.

The flat, though colourful, is cheaply furnished.

There's a knock at the door.

BEATRICE (O.O.S.): Is only me.

Eldridge heaves himself up, unlocks three locks on the door and lets her in. Ethnic glances at the shopping bag.

(Note: When not among whites, Ethnic speaks in Anglo-Jamaican speech rhythms and vernacular).

ETHNIC: I coulda carry that fo' you ...

BEATRICE: Yeah, is what I did think ...

ETHNIC: Cup of tea?

BEATRICE: (*making straight for the kitchen*) I'll do it.

ELDRIDGE: You wan me fo do it?

56

BEATRICE: Eldridge, I waited twenty-five years for that day. I can wait another twenty-five.
Ethnic moves to take her shopping bag. She tugs it away.
BEATRICE: Is okay. T'ain't heavy or nuttin.
Ethnic looks at her suspiciously, as she continues into the kitchen.

68. INT. ETHNIC'S PARENTS' KITCHEN. DAY
It's basic, run-down, with wooden slats across the window. Beatrice enters, plonks down her shopping bag and starts filling the kettle.
(INTERCUT, *as required, between Kitchen and Living Room*).
BEATRICE: Is wha a go on out dere?
ELDRIDGE: Is how me fo know? You is the one who was out a street.
BEATRICE: There's a whole heap of police out dere. Bobbylan everywhere. The place a crawl with dem bobbylan.
ETHNIC: (*suspiciously*) Ma? *Why* ain't de shoppin' bag heavy?
BEATRICE: They na knock pon no doors or nuttin . . .
ELDRIDGE: Hallelujah, the whole place fall down . . .
ETHNIC: Ma? You only got half de shoppin' again?
No reply from Beatrice. Ethnic and Eldridge exchange a wry look, Ethnic puts down the iron and walks to the kitchen, shaking his head in weary irritation.

69. INT. KITCHEN. DAY. CONTINUOUS
Beatrice avoids Ethnic's look of disapproval, as he walks in. She starts unpacking the groceries.
ETHNIC: Ma. You have to cut it out. I keep tellin' yo.
BEATRICE: (*evasively*) En't you got some bony knees . . . ?
ETHNIC: Goin back a street to de shops ten times don't fool no one.

57

BEATRICE: (*calling*) Eldridge? Who these knees take after? T'ain't my side ...
Ethnic tugs the issue-evading groceries from her and slams them down on the table, then shakes his head at her like an indulgent parent.

ETHNIC: There's nuttin be ashamed of gettin all your shoppin in one go ...

BEATRICE: Mrs Green was in, and Mrs Mead and old Mr Winston. I can't go flash money about on cornflakes and jam and stuff in front of them. Maryland Cookies. They got their pride.

ETHNIC: Mrs Green knows your boy hold a job! They known for years!

ELDRIDGE (O.O.S.): Dey doan know *what* job ...
Some don't.

ETHNIC: *Any* job!

BEATRICE: You tell 'em that wit all dem bobbylan a knock their door down ...

ETHNIC: You said they *wasn't* knockin' no doors ... !
An uncomfortable pause.

BEATRICE: I'll go back when the shop more got no people in. You have to think of folks' feeling.
There's a sudden heavy knocking on the door. Beatrice and Eldridge stiffen apprehensively. Ethnic looks at them.

ETHNIC: What the panic? You two dealin' in herbs? What yo bin pushin, Ma? Tate and Lyle? Jesus ... !
He exits.

70. INT. LIVING ROOM. CONTINUOUS. DAY
Ethnic makes his way from the kitchen.

BEATRICE: (*calling, O.O.S.*) Put ya pants on!
Ethnic struggles into his pants as he goes to the door. Another couple of knocks. He opens the door.

71. EXT. DOORSTEP PARENTS' FLAT. CONTINUOUS.
DAY
*Ethnic's fellow Ghetto Blasters are on the doorstep,
with their instrument cases. Ethnic's face falls.*
CLAUDE: Alright, den, Spar?
ETHNIC: Hey, we didn't fix nothing, did we?
LLOYD: Ole man! We arrange it. Rehearsal.
ETHNIC: Shit, man! I got a weddin to go to . . .
LLOYD: Tell 'em to have it tomorrow . . .
ETHNIC: Forgot, didn't I?
LLOYD: No sweat.
ETHNIC: Cool runnings.
MAXWELL: Later.
    They leave. Ethnic closes the door.

72. EXT. BALCONY OF FLATS. CONTINUOUS DAY
*Two policemen are standing at the top of the stairs, as
Claude, Maxwell and Lloyd make their way down.
With exaggerated wryness, the Ghetto Blasters open
their instrument cases before they've even reached the
policemen. They show their innocent instruments to the
police as they pass.*
CLAUDE: All clean, Mr Pig, all clean.
1ST P.C: Mr What?
LLOYD: Big. Mr Big.
1ST P.C: Move along.
*They do so – and descend the stairs, fastening their
cases as they go. Two more policemen are waiting,
watching them. As they approach . . .*
3RD P.C: Open up.
LLOYD: We just showed them two!
3RD P.C: Show *me*.
*Wearily, they start to open their instrument cases
again.*

73. A FRAMED PHOTOGRAPH
*of a young woman and a six year old girl, smiling
happily in C.U., their heads together.*
PULL BACK *to see we're . . .*

74. INT. BAYLEAF'S BEDROOM. DAY
*The photograph is on the bedside, beside a phone. The
bed is unmade – but only one half of it has been slept
in.
Bayleaf's clothes are lying in dishevelled heaps on the
floor. The washing basket is overflowing. There are no
signs of a woman's presence in the room – which seems
half furnished.
Bayleaf is dressed for the wedding in his best suit.
He's seated on the edge of the bed, sewing a button on
his shirt (without taking the jacket off).
The phone rings. He swivels round, tensely. Then
dashes and grabs it.*
BAYLEAF: (*into phone*) Hello? (*beat, then excitedly*)

Karen? (*beat; his excitement evaporates*) Oh,
morning, Mrs Webb. Sorry I won't be with you –
I've a wedding to go to, so tomorrow's ...
(*pause*) You can't have gone off the Sudden
Sunset ... I've done the whole under-coat and ...
(*pause*) I expect your daughter's boyfriend thinks
the Golden Aubergine, does he? (*pause*) Oh,
well, he *is* a Computer Engineer. He'll know ...

75. INT. TATE'S HOUSE: CONSERVATORY EXTENSION.
DAY
*Tate is seated at a table, working on his model of Ally
Pally. Tongue bulging out his cheek in concentration.*
   *His wife, Nancy, comes in from the kitchen, carrying
a mug of tea and a cheese and onion roll on a tray. She
has murder in her eyes.*
TATE: Careful. It's a tricky bit, this. Don't bang the

tray. (*She promptly slams the tray down hard next to the model.*) Nancy!!

NANCY: How many times do we get to go *anywhere* together! Let alone . . .

TATE: *Cats*, Christmas 1983.

NANCY: Let alone a *wedding*! How many times are we even *off-duty* at the same time!

Tate leans back from his model with exaggerated patience.

TATE: Nancy, it's not a normal wedding . . .

NANCY: We didn't get *in* to *Cats*. The nearest you could park was Shaftesbury Avenue. We finished up at A24 Soho. Having a cup of tea with Red Watch . . .

TATE: Nancy. I've been to *two* of his bloody weddings already. They're not normal. *He's* not normal. He only got divorced *yesterday*.

NANCY: A wedding's a wedding. A man on your own watch. It's unheard of.

From out in the street, we hear the sirens of a passing Fire Vehicle on its way to a job. Tate listens with excited interest.

TATE: Harry's lot. Pump only. Nothing special. (*looks at his watch*) Bang in the middle of stand-easy. (*laughs*) They're missing their cheese and onion rolls. . .

NANCY: He's always seemed very normal to *me*.

TATE:(*incredulous*) Vaseline?

NANCY: Compared to some you've had.

TATE: He's different with you.

NANCY: So are *you*.

TATE: Sorry?

NANCY: You're like a Cabbage-Patch Doll with Blue Watch. With me you're a Station Officer.

TATE: There's no reception. No wedding breakfast. There isn't even a honeymoon. He's even coming on watch tonight . . .

She starts to go. He looks at his tray.

Where's my other cheese and onion? You always
give me two ...

NANCY: (*over her shoulder*) It's *Bayleaf* who gives you
two.

TATE: And you.

NANCY: (*exiting*) Not any more.

TATE: And where's my H.P.!!

76. EXT. STREET. DAY
*A woman barges her way purposefully, angrily,
through other pedestrians, to a local register office. She
stops at a noticeboard at the door – which indicates the
room numbers of the various departments – then
crashes her way in. This is Vaseline's ex-wife, Marion I.*

77. INT. 'MARRIAGE ROOM' REGISTRAR'S OFFICE. DAY
The ceremony is just beginning. Facing the registrar are

Vaseline and his bride, Marion II. Grouped behind
them are Bayleaf, Ethnic, Rambo, Charisma, Malcolm
and friends or relatives of the bride.

REGISTRAR: Now who has the ring, please?

MARION II: My Dad.

REGISTRAR: Yes – and who exactly *is* your –
Marion II turns to her father, standing in the
group.

MARION II: Dad. Now.
He's about to hand her the ring.

REGISTRAR: Would you place it on the cushion,
please.

MARION II: (*to Dad*) On the cushion.

VASELINE: On the cushion.
Dad places it on the cushion.

REGISTRAR: Now, Roland, repeat this declaration
after me . . .
Ethnic nudges Bayleaf.

ETHNIC: 'Roland'?? I never knew he was a Roland!

BAYLEAF: Well, he can't have been christened
Vaseline, can he? It's advertising.

REGISTRAR: (*reading from small card*) 'I do solemnly
declare . . .'

VASELINE: (*piously*) I do solemnly declare . . .

REGISTRAR: 'That I know not of any lawful
impediment . . .'

VASELINE: That I know not of any lawful
impediment . . .

REGISTRAR: 'Why I, Roland Oliver (*Ethnic almost*
dissolves) may not be joined in matrimony . . .'

VASELINE: Why I, Roland Oliver Cartwright, may not
be . . .
Marion I bursts in.

MARION I: No, but *I* do, don't I! I pigging do!
The Registrar boggles. Everyone else swivels
round to gape at her.

VASELINE: (*horrified*) Oh, hell . . .

MARION I: (*to* MARION II) You marry a fireman, you

stupid cow, you'll never be joined in nothing!
You'll never bloody *see* him! You'll . . .

REGISTRAR: Excuse me, madam –

MARION I: You want a lawful impediment, mister? (*re Vaseline*) He's one! (*re the others*) *And* them! All of 'em! They have fancy women ringing 999 in the middle of the night, just for a bit of . . .

MARION II: Well, you ought to *bloody* know! That's how you nailed him in the *first* place!

REGISTRAR: Madam, would you kindly . . .

BAYLEAF: (*to his mates*) Blue Watch! As detailed! One-arm-lift! Go!
They form a wall and hustle Marion I out of the room. Marion II gives Vaseline a dirty look.

VASELINE: Well, don't look at me. *I* didn't invite her!

REGISTRAR: Can we get on with as little hysteria as possible, please? I've a Jew and a Catholic booked in at twelve . . .

78. INT. JOSIE'S HOUSE: BATHROOM. DAY
Josie is in the bath with her husband, Gerry. He's sitting with his back to her. She's shampooing his hair. She's prattling on happily. He's gone from uninterested to irritated.

JOSIE: . . . and according to Bayleaf, he's called Vaseline because he's always got a bit on the side . . .

GERRY: I don't get it.

JOSIE: Apart from always getting married . . .

GERRY: I still don't get it.

JOSIE: 'Vaseline'.

GERRY: Soap in my eyes. Towel.
She hands him a towel. He rubs at one of his eyes.

JOSIE: Sick Note's Sick Note because he's the top skate. Always on light duties. Trying to work his ticket, really, according to Bayleaf, 'cos his pension's . . .

GERRY: Why is Bayleaf Bayleaf?

65

JOSIE: He's the Mess Manager for the Watch.

GERRY: I don't get it.

JOSIE: He does the cooking.

GERRY: (*a beat*) What *is* a Bayleaf?

JOSIE: It goes in cooking.

GERRY: Here.

He hands back the towel.

JOSIE: Then there's Rambo. According to Bayleaf, Rambo's –

GERRY: There's a lot of according to Bayleaf, isn't there?

JOSIE: (*a beat*) How d'you mean?

GERRY: Don't you get no fires to put out, you two?

An uncomfortable pause.

JOSIE: (*flatly*) Apart from Ethnic, he's the only one who's said a word to me so far.

GERRY: (*pointedly*) Oh, yes?

66

JOSIE: (*angrily*) Oh, for Christ's sake!
A silence. She starts towelling his rinsed hair. He grabs the towel from her and starts doing it for himself.
GERRY: Girl behind the counter at the Job Centre. *She* has a nickname. (*Josie ignores him*). 'Little Darling', we call her. Know why? (*Josie grabs a bath towel and gets splashily out of the bath.*) 'Cos she en't always blabbing about bleedin' Bay Leaves. Get it?
Josie slams out of the door.

79. INT. DOCTOR'S SURGERY. DAY
Sick Note is seated with his shirt off and one trouser-leg rolled up. The doctor is bending low, or kneeling, in front of him, prodding his knee.
    He then returns to his desk, sits down and writes a

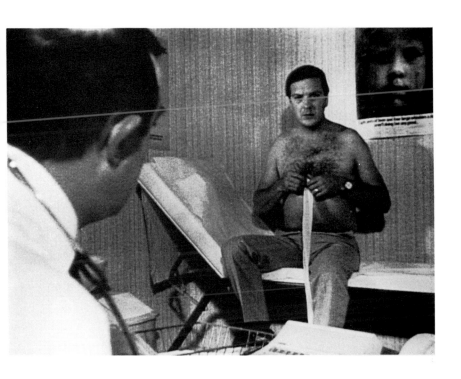

note on Sick Note's file. He then closes the file, looks at
Sick Note and sighs.
DOCTOR: I've got some bad news. I think you'd better
    brace yourself.
SICK NOTE: Oh, yes?
DOCTOR: I can't give you a sick note.
SICK NOTE: Sorry?
DOCTOR: There's nothing wrong with you.
SICK NOTE: What – *any*where?
DOCTOR: You'll adjust to it in time. It's something
    you'll have to learn to accept and live with.
    (*presses intercom*) Next!
SICK NOTE: Have I told you about my headaches?
DOCTOR: One day I'll tell you about mine . . .

80. INT. MRS GRANT'S KITCHEN. DAY
Mrs Grant is peeling potatoes at the sink. Through the
window in front of her, we see the back garden
and burnt-out shell of what was once the garden
shed.
  Suddenly a movement catches her eye. She peers,
uncertainly, through the window. And sees Vaseline,
already in his gardening clothes, beginning work on the
flower bed.
  She immediately stops peeling, wipes her hands on
her pinny and starts for the door.

81. EXT. MRS GRANT'S BACK GARDEN. DAY
Vaseline is planting. The door of the back porch opens
and Mrs Grant appears. She calls from the doorstep.
MRS GRANT: Excuse me! Are you there?
    Vaseline turns.
I thought you were getting married today?
VASELINE: That's right.
    A puzzled beat.
MRS GRANT: Well . . . um . . . why are you . . . um . . .
    what are you . . . ?

VASELINE: Bit of a barney.

MRS GRANT: Already??

VASELINE: Oh, not the wife. The wife and my *other* wife.

MRS GRANT: (*struggling*) First wife.

VASELINE: Second wife. The first one's a customs officer in Hull, Yorkshire.

MRS GRANT: (*sorry she ever started*) Ah.

VASELINE: Well, Humberside they call it now.

MRS GRANT: Oh, do they? (*beat*) Um . . . my husband's decided to do his *own* gardening in future . . .

A beat.

VASELINE: Oh. (*beat*) Right, then.

MRS GRANT: No disrespect.

VASELINE: No.

MRS GRANT: Um . . . excuse me asking . . . um . . . are you by any chance a *fireman*, exactly?

VASELINE: In what way?

MRS GRANT: (*dismissing it*) No, no . . . it's just . . . well, thank you anyway. Goodbye, then.

She starts to go in.

VASELINE: Have you got that quid you owe me?

MRS GRANT: (*politely*) Oh . . . I wouldn't insult you.

VASELINE: (*bemused*) No. Right.

She goes in.

82. EXT. GHETTO FLATS. DAY

More police transport vehicles and more patrolling policemen very much in evidence.

Two policemen are at the door of one of the flats. One of them hammers hard on the door. A young black woman opens it, a baby in her arms. More children can be heard inside.

IST P.C: Routine inquiry.

YOUNG WOMAN: Yeah, is what I hear tell. 'Have I had a TV delivered?'

IST P.C: That's right.

YOUNG WOMAN: If I could afford a licence I'd get a telly, alright?

2ND P.C: Have you had a TV delivered, yes or no?

YOUNG WOMAN: (*to 1st P.C.*) This feller understan English?

1ST P.C: (*to colleague*) Come on.

2ND P.C: (*to young woman*) Do you know anybody who *has* had one delivered?

YOUNG WOMAN: If I did, d'you think I'd be stupid enough to tell?

2ND P.C: What?

YOUNG WOMAN: I'd get my face cut 'fore I even open my mouth . . . Look at the doors roun' here . . . you see one that en't been smashed in? T'ain't ordinary folk you're lookin for, mister. T'ain't even folk who live here.

1ST P.C: (*to colleague*) Come on.

They walk away. The young woman closes the door.

83. ANOTHER PART OF THE GHETTO. DAY

Ethnic, carrying his carrier-bag with his undress uniform inside, comes out of his parents' flat and starts to make his way along the balcony to the staircase.

   Two policemen are making their way along the balcony, knocking on doors.

84. P.O.V. OF THE ABOVE

From the window of a higher flat – where the two Rastas and Whitey are standing watching.

   They see the policemen stop Ethnic, make him open his carrier-bag, acknowledge his innocence amicably, then let him go on his way.

1ST RASTA: I doan think he have a real job. There's somethin' weird. I reckon he a stripper up West or somethin'.

2ND RASTA: Nah. He work daytime too, some days.

WHITEY: Yeah, well, they're dirty bastards up West, en't they?

1ST RASTA: I tell you, man. There's somethin' weird *somewhere* . . .

85. INT. LOCKER ROOM. FIRE STATION. NIGHT
Charisma opens his locker – the inside doors of which are plastered with photos of snooker celebrities – and starts taking out the slithering packets of bacon.

86. INT. CORRIDOR. NIGHT
Charisma walks along. As he passes the Rest Room door, he pops his head in, to see . . .

87. INT. REST ROOM CONTINUOUS. NIGHT
Bayleaf and Malcolm at one side of the coffee table. Rambo and Ethnic on the other. They're in the middle of a game of Trivial Pursuit.
Josie stands – excluded as usual – at the other side of the room, going through the motions of skimming through the London Evening Standard.
Bayleaf looks at where Ethnic's counter has landed.

BAYLEAF: Right, Geography, is it?

ETHNIC: Is it?

RAMBO: No, no!
He moves the counter in the opposite direction. Go *this* way. You want Arts and Literature . . .

ETHNIC: (*dubiously*) Do I?

CHARISMA: 'Scuse me, Bayleaf, you got a minute?
Bayleaf – and the others – ignore him.

BAYLEAF: (*To Ethnic*) Arts and Literature then?

ETHNIC: Yeah, alright, go on.
Charisma withdraws his head.

BAYLEAF: (*reading from card*) What was George Sand's relationship with Chopin?

RAMBO: Um . . . brother-in-law.

BAYLEAF: (*reading the answer*) She was his mistress.

RAMBO: Oh . . . *that* Chopin . . .!

71

88. INT. MESS/KITCHEN CONTINUOUS, NIGHT
Charisma enters with his packets of bacon. Vaseline
and Hallam are playing pontoon at the table. The
phone rings (behind Hallam).
VASELINE: (*jumping*) If it's either of 'em, I'm out on a
shout, alright? A six-pumper at a Marriage
Guidance Clinic. And I'm pouring petrol on the
bastard.
Hallam takes the phone.
HALLAM: (*into phone*) Pig sty. (*beat*) Vaseline . . . it's
for . . .
HALLAM/CHARISMA: (*as Charisma makes his way to*
the kitchen) – Yoo, hoo!
VASELINE: (*seething, to Hallam*) I just told you I'm
not here!
HALLAM: (*beams, offers phone*) Reverse charge from
Hull, Humberside . . .

89. INT. REST ROOM CONTINUOUS. NIGHT
Bayleaf, Malcolm, Ethnic and Rambo still playing
Trivial Pursuit. Josie still reading.
BAYLEAF: Well?
ETHNIC: I don't know.
MALCOLM: Guess.
ETHNIC: I've never heard of Marlene Dietrich!
BAYLEAF: Here y'are, then. I'll give you another.
MALCOLM: You can't do that!
BAYLEAF: What's Nat King Cole got twice what
Jimmy White's got?
ETHNIC: You what??
BAYLEAF/JOSIE: Black balls.
They all swivel round to stare at her. Her response
had been totally automatic. She smiles weakly.
JOSIE: Sorry.
Charisma pops his head round the door again.
CHARISMA: (*with appallingly unconvincing*
nonchalance) It's in the fridge, by the way.
BAYLEAF: Sorry?

CHARISMA: The bacon. (*Bayleaf looks baffled.*) The
    bacon is in the fridge.
BAYLEAF: (*a beat*) Is that some kind of password?
CHARISMA: Eh?
BAYLEAF: Pardon?
CHARISMA: That I promised you. From my mate. The
    bacon contact.
BAYLEAF: (*with exaggerated comprehension*) Oh!
    With you! With you!

90. INT. MESS/KITCHEN. DAY
Open on the packets of bacon. Bayleaf is examining
them, with assumed gratitude and incredulity.
    Charisma watches with immense fulfilment.
BAYLEAF: 91p?
CHARISMA: Might even be cheaper next time . . .
BAYLEAF: Must be one *hell* of a mate . . .
    This is one of the happiest moments of Charisma's
    life.
CHARISMA: I just have to say the word . . .
    He shrugs modestly and wanders away. Bayleaf
    starts replacing the packets in the fridge. He notices
    that one of them still has its price tag and the name
    of the mini-market. With a glance to check that
    Charisma is out of sight, he scratches the label off
    and throws it away. He puts the packet in the
    fridge and closes the door.

91. INT. FIRE BRIGADE CONTROL CENTRE CROYDON.
NIGHT
Four operators, wearing headsets, sit at VDU screens. A
2nd operator per VDU screen stands by – also in headset
– monitoring and manning 'index drums'.
    Three or four Brigade Officers are busy at desks.
About half the total personnel are women.
    In front of the four operators, alarm lights almost
incessantly light up. The operator then takes the call

*(via British Telecom), ascertains the caller's address,
and types out the information on the* VDU.

*Simultaneously, the 2nd operator (who's also
connected to the call) takes the grid reference from the
index drum and passes the relevant information to the*
VDU *operator.*

*He or she then punches the appropriate button on a
control panel – which rings the bells in the fire station
nearest to the caller's address.*

Nancy Tate is one of the VDU *operators.*

*We watch two or three calls come in – almost without
interval. Another arrives. Nancy takes it (she types at
the* VDU *throughout).*

NANCY: Fire Brigade. (*beat – British Telecom gives
caller's number*) Fire Brigade. (*beat*) What's the
problem? (*beat*) You're trapped in your flat.
(*beat*) What's your address? (*She types the*

information on to the VDU *screen as it comes in,
then reads back.*) That's Flat 3, Egerton Court,
James Street, S.E.1 (*Beat*) Don't worry sir, we're
on our way.
2ND OPERATOR: (*re index info*)
45 Q2 83 B25 Pump N.T. 12.54 (*Nancy types this
on her computer.*) Your Sydney's getting a
bellyful tonight.
NANCY: Serves him right.
She punches the telex panel button.
IMMEDIATE CUT TO:

92. INT./EXT. FIRE STATION. NIGHT
*a) Watchroom. The bells go down. 'Pump only' lights
flash.
b) Yard. Tate, Bayleaf, Ethnic, Vaseline and Josie leap
into the pump.
It hurtles out into the night, sirens sounding, lights
flashing.*

93. INT. CORRIDOR EGERTON COURT FLATS. NIGHT
*Tate, Ethnic and Vaseline approach the door with axes.
Bayleaf and Josie stand by at the entrance of the
building with bottles of compressed air, a length of
electric cable and heavy cutting equipment.
A neighbour pops his head out of the door of another
flat as Ethnic is passing.*
NEIGHBOUR: Always *something*, isn't there?
ETHNIC: Sorry?
NEIGHBOUR: If it isn't one thing, it's another.
ETHNIC: Right.
NEIGHBOUR: Still, I suppose, if we'd nothing to
grumble about, we'd grumble ...
ETHNIC: (*trying to get away*) 'Scuse me.
NEIGHBOUR: I once slept next to a fireman outside
Selfridges. We were waiting for 'em to open for
the January sales.
ETHNIC: Shows you.

TATE *hammers on the door of Flat 3.*

TATE: (*calling*) London Fire Brigade! Can anyone hear? Hello? Fire Brigade?

VASELINE: Shall I smash the bugger down?

MAN'S VOICE: (*from inside*) Hang on, I'll let you in . . .

Ethnic turns to Tate, puzzled.

ETHNIC: I thought he was trapped?

TATE: Might not be him. Could be his missus. In a rabbit-snare.

VASELINE: I must ask him where he got it.

The door opens. A man appears, naked apart from a towel round his waist.

TATE: Right, sir. Where's the person?

MAN: (*beside himself with embarrassment*) Um . . . here.

TATE: The person *trapped*, sir.

MAN: Yes. Me.

A puzzled beat.

VASELINE: You're bloody *not*, though!

MAN: (*almost in tears*) I ... I should've just gone to the hospital, by rights ... I couldn't, though ... I mean, not with *nurses* around, and that ... you feel a fool, don't you?

TATE: I'm sorry, sir, I don't quite under ...

MAN: Come in ... I'll show you ... we're all men of the world ...

He leads them into his flat, closing the door behind them.

We stay on Bayleaf and Josie at the entrance. A beat.

JOSIE: How were your days off?

BAYLEAF: Fine. Yours?

JOSIE: Yeah.

A pause.

BAYLEAF: Bit quiet, really. Karen done a bunk four months ago. The wife. Took the kid with her. Melanie. I've never told the lads ... The guv'nor knows. But that's all.

She stares at him.

JOSIE: You've never told the lads?

BAYLEAF: You can't tell firemen things like that. Not unless they've brought a change of underpants. (*A beat. He suddenly looks at her.*) What the hell am I telling *you* for?

94. INT. FLAT 3. NIGHT

The man, with his back to us, is now completely naked – the towel round his ankles. Tate, Ethnic and Vaseline are grouped in front of him, staring in disbelief at his loins.

A pause.

TATE: A curtain ring?

MAN: P'raps I should've called an ambulance ...

TATE: How the hell've you got a curtain ring stuck on your ... (*to Ethnic*) Get Bayleaf.

Ethnic goes.

VASELINE: Just fell off the curtain rail, did it, and happened to fall right on your –

MAN: It won't come off. I've been like this for ...

ETHNIC (O.O.S.): (*calling*) Bayleaf! Bolt cropper, please!

MAN: (*apprehensively*) What's a bolt-cropper?

Tate and Vaseline are scared of looking at each other, in case they laugh. Ethnic and Bayleaf, lugging heavy cutting equipment, enter. Bayleaf stops dead on seeing the problem. He looks at the others. They all avoid his eyes – and each other's.

BAYLEAF: Um ...

MAN: What do you think?

BAYLEAF: Well, off the top of my head ... Have you ever thought of joining a circus?

MAN: It's jammed ... It's bloody strangling me ...

Bayleaf examines the huge cutters, whistling thoughtfully.

VASELINE: (*calling*) Firewoman Ingham! Come here!

TATE: Are you bloody barmy!

ETHNIC: No. Evil.

MAN: Did he say Fire*woman*??

TATE: (*calling*) It's all right, Ingham. No need to –

Too late. Josie races in. The men part, so that she gets a good view of what exactly is trapped. She stops dead. The man embarrassedly covers himself with his hands.

MAN: It's alright ... forget it ... It'll drop off in time.

JOSIE: You can say that again.

MAN: No, I mean the –

JOSIE: (*rolling her sleeves up*) Have you got any ice?

MAN: What?

JOSIE: In the fridge. Ice. Frozen water. Ice cubes. To reduce your ... um ... swelling.

MAN: Hang on.

*He grabs the towel, wraps it around himself and
goes to the kitchen.*
Josie turns to Vaseline.
JOSIE: Having a better honeymoon than you, inn'e?
DISSOLVE TO:

95. INT. MESS/KITCHEN. NIGHT
*Josie is making herself a mug of tea. Then, one by one,
into the Mess troop Sick Note, Charisma – snooker cue
in hand– Rambo and Malcolm, followed by Bayleaf,
Ethnic and Vaseline, together.*
  *They all stand framed in the hatch, looking at her
like guilty schoolboys. She looks levelly back at them.*
JOSIE: One lousy joke about that last shout, just one,
    and . . .
MALCOLM: (*with embarrassed deference*) No . . . we

79

just wanted to say . . . um . . . on behalf of Blue
Watch . . . we think you're O.K.

JOSIE: (*beat*) Well, that's all right, then.

RAMBO: Any chance of a cuppa Josie?

JOSIE: Ask Bayleaf, it's his kitchen.

*She walks past them into the Mess, with the
slightest of grins at Bayleaf – and sits at the table
with her mug of tea. Turns over a paperback and
starts reading.*

MALCOLM: We'll have to think of a nickname for you
now.

RAMBO: How about the Ice Maiden?

*The others look at him with newly found gallant
distaste.*

VASELINE: (*to the others, disgustedly*) Tasteless,
inn'e? Crude bugger. No respect at all . . .

96. A TERRACED HOUSE – BLAZING FIERCELY. NIGHT

*This is a major fire. An inferno. We hear screams.
Crashing masonry. People outside watch in helpless
horror. We hear the wail of approaching sirens.*

97. EXT. STREET. NIGHT

*The pump-ladder hurtling along – lights flashing, sirens
wailing. Careering behind it comes the pump.*

98. INT. PUMP. NIGHT

*Bayleaf, driving. Beside him is Tate. Behind them are
Ethnic, Josie and Vaseline changing into their
firefighting gear. Vaseline cocks an ear at the sirens.*

VASELINE: That's it! How about Ring-a-Ding?

JOSIE: Eh?

VASELINE: Your nickname.

JOSIE: How about Josie?

VASELINE: Ring-a-*Dong*! Even better! Bloody Ring-
a-*Dong*! Do you get it?!

JOSIE: Um . . .this *respect* you were on about . . .
Didn't last long, did it?
VASELINE: That was for public consumption . . . This
is on our own.
ETHNIC: You're not *on* your own. *I'm* here.
VASELINE: Oh, sorry, son, didn't see you. I thought
you were a shadow.
*Ethnic makes to thump him. Vaseline strikes back.
Josie restrains them both.*
JOSIE: Hey! Hey! Cut it out! Right now! (*They do
so.*)

99. EXT. TERRACED HOUSE. NIGHT
*The fire has now an even stronger grip. The pump and
pump-ladder speed towards it. A police car speeds in
the opposite direction.*

100. INT./EXT. PUMP CAB CONTINUOUS. NIGHT
Tate and Bayleaf see the fire through the windscreen, as Bayleaf brakes outside the house.
TATE: Jesus Christ!
BAYLEAF: (*into R/T*) B251 and B252, status 3. Over.
Hallam appears – running to them from the scene of the fire. He yells through Tate's opening door.
HALLAM: Two – maybe three – inside. It's a go-er.
TATE: (*to Bayleaf*) Make Pump four. Persons reported.
He leaps out of the cabin.

101. A MONTAGE. NIGHT
a) INT. HOUSE: *Members of Blue Watch, trying to negotiate the ferociously burning, collapsing staircase, hosing as they go.*

b) EXT. HOUSE: *Hoses play on the flames from every angle.*
   An ambulance and police car are in attendance. The air is filled with the sound of crashing walls, the roar of flames, the rush of water.
Josie is now working with the team – all of them efficiently, purposefully and bravely battling the fire.
c) INT. HOUSE: *smoke billows out from under the door; working in pairs, the team smash down the door. They tread warily into a black, smoke-filled room. They hear cries. They walk round the perimeter of the room, hands feeling the walls, towards the cries. The ceiling collapses.*
d) EXT. HOUSE: *Hallam and another, wearing breathing apparatus comes out, carrying a screaming, badly burned child.*
   Ambulance men rush to assist.
e) INT. HOUSE: *On the landing, Vaseline and another in breathing apparatus, struggle against the smoke and flame to reach a child's bedroom. (Name plate on the door reading Linda.)*
   The floor collapses. Vaseline falls partially through it. Others reach him, haul him up and away. Another opens Linda's door.
   Inside, a flashover hurtles a huge, swirling ball of flame through the blackness towards the door. Malcolm's clothes ignite.
f) EXT. HOUSE: *The first child is being attended to by ambulance men.*
   Rambo drags Vaseline out of the house. Tate races across to him. Malcolm gets out – hurt – but carrying another child, a small boy. Josie grabs the boy, gives him mouth-to-mouth resuscitation till the ambulance men take over.
   Tate moves away from a knot of neighbours and yells at the team.
TATE: One more in there, lads! Another kid!
   Bayleaf rams on his breathing apparatus and goes into the house, with another fireman.

102. CORNER OF THE SAME STREET. NIGHT
*Two women, in their thirties, stroll around the corner,
laughing together, arm in arm. They see the fire, the
vehicles, the crowd – and their faces freeze. Particularly
1st Woman ... at first apprehensive ... then
increasingly, horrifyingly certain that it's her house.*
1ST WOMAN: What's ... Oh, Christ, no ... Oh, God,
    don't let it be my ... please, please, God, don't
    let it ...
    *She starts to run, faster and faster towards the
    house.*

103. EXT. TERRACED HOUSE CONTINUOUS. NIGHT
*Bayleaf comes out of the house, carrying a small corpse
in his arms. He walks slowly away from the house.
Tate rushes up to him and frees him from his breathing
apparatus.*

The corpse is that of a six-year-old girl – naked,
blackened.
1st Woman races up, seeing first one screaming child
being bundled into an ambulance by ambulance men,
then another, and now the obscene horror of the third.
She stops. Stares at it and starts screaming helplessly.
A policewoman tries to put an arm round her. She
throws it off.

104. INT. TERRACED HOUSE. NIGHT
The lads are hosing the now subsiding fire. Room by
room is gradually revealed, through the rivers of water,
as burnt-out, melted, grotesque ruins.

105. EXT. TERRACED HOUSE. NIGHT
1st Woman is in shock. She's being attended to by
policewomen and ambulance men.
  A group of neighbours stands near by. Silent. Some
of them weeping.
  The corpse is covered by a plastic sheet.
  Suddenly, Bayleaf, maniacally crashes through the
circle surrounding 1st Woman, and tries to grab her.
BAYLEAF: 'Disco'? You went off to a bleeding disco!!
  Three kids on their own! (*The others try to*
  restrain him. Tate and Hallam run towards them.)
  Well, there's only *two* now, isn't there!! Burnt to
  buggery! For bleeding life! The little un's a lump
  of melted cheese!!
Tate and Hallam, dishevelled, exhausted,
blackened and burned manage to pull him away.
1ST WOMAN: Once a fortnight . . . that's all . . .
  one night out . . . nothing's ever happened before
  . . . Nothing . . . Oh, God, . . . God, in heaven . . .
BAYLEAF: (*between Tate and Hallam – some feet away*
  from her) Dancing . . . she went dancing . . .
He pulls away from Tate and Hallam, turns away,
staring into the night.

85

*Josie, at the pump, watches him, as she gets into
her breathing apparatus.*

ANGLE ON NEIGHBOURS
An elderly woman stands weeping.

ELDERLY WOMAN: He shouldn't do that ... She's the
mother ... he has no right ...
A middle-aged man stands next to her.

MIDDLE-AGED MAN: It's when it's kids. It's the one
thing they can't take ... when it's kids ...
*Bayleaf turns back again. A dead moment, then he
automatically starts reconnecting his breathing
apparatus.
Josie glances at Tate for his okay – and goes into
the house with Bayleaf.*

106. EXT. STREET LONG SHOT. DAWN IS BREAKING
*The firemen still working. Everyone else has gone – the
residents, ambulance men, the police. A silence.*
DISSOLVE TO:

107. EXT. LONDON STREETS. DAWN
*The two machines driving back to the station. No lights
or sirens. The streets deserted.*

108. INT. PUMP (TRAVELLING). DAWN
*A dead silence. Everyone staring ahead. They all look
drained, their uniforms stained, burned, torn.
Vaseline is nursing his leg. After a few moments ...*
VASELINE: I'm losing a lot of blood.
ETHNIC: No, you're not. It's going in your boots.
*No smiles. No reactions of any kind. The exchange
is entirely automatic. They ride on in silence.*

109. INT. WATCHROOM. DAWN
*Sick Note sits in silence. Hallam is typing out the fire
report.*

110. INT. TATE'S OFFICE. DAWN
Tate is seated at his desk. Glances at the model of Ally
Pally. Pushes it to one side. Sits in silence.

111. INT. REST ROOM, DAWN
Rambo sits in silence, looking at the blank screen of the
TV set, stroking the cat in his lap.

112. INT. RECREATION ROOM. DAWN
The snooker balls on the table as they were left hours
earlier.
Charisma sits in silence.

113. INT. DORMITORY. DAWN
Malcolm and Vaseline lying on their beds in silence.

114. INT. MESS/KITCHEN. DAWN
Ethnic and Josie sit in silence. Josie is warming her hands round a mug of tea.
  She slides Ethnic's untouched mug closer to him. He nods fractional acknowledgement. But still doesn't touch it.
  After a moment, she gets up and walks slowly from the room.

115. INT. FIRE STATION APPLIANCE ROOM. DAWN
The two machines stand silent. Bayleaf is seated on the tailboard of the pump, not moving, just staring ahead.
  Josie approaches him from the building. She sits beside him. A pause.
JOSIE: (*quietly*) I think you should tell the lads. About your wife and kid.
  A silence.
  At least your kid's alive. 'S'all that matters in the end. Everything else is bonus . . .
  They sit, staring ahead.
  Over the silence, at first very softly, then growing gradually louder and louder, we hear V.O., the sound of one child's voice – then more and more – singing in a round . . .
CHILDREN'S VOICES: London's burning
  London's burning
  Call the engine
  Call the engine
  Fire, fire
  Fire, fire
  Pour on water
  Pour on water
  As the round continues . . .
  DISSOLVE TO:

116. EXT. INNER CITY JUNIOR COMPREHENSIVE SCHOOL PLAYGROUND. DAY
The pump is parked. Standing beside it in firefighting

uniform are Hallam, Bayleaf and Ethnic, facing a group of schoolchildren and their teacher.
   These are the children singing the round. They continue singing it. Hallam, Bayleaf and Ethnic listen, trying to fight the tedium by looking as appreciative and indulgent as they can.
   Outside the school gates, other, older, kids are fooling aimlessly around.
   The singing finally comes to an end. Hallam, Bayleaf and Ethnic clap a little embarrassedly.
HALLAM: Thank you, children. Very nice.
BAYLEAF: He's impressed.
   The teacher addresses the kids.
TEACHER: Right. Now on behalf of all of us, Dominic here will say thank you for bringing your fire engine to the school and showing us how everything works. Dominic.

DOMINIC: What?

TEACHER: Go on.

DOMINIC: (*to firemen*) Thank you.

Hallam, Bayleaf and Ethnic manage another appreciative smile.

HALLAM: Thank *you*, Dominic. And do you want to drive a fire engine when you grow up?

DOMINIC: No, a Jaguar XJS like my dad.

Watching all this, wry and bored – then suddenly intently – is one of the kids outside the railings. He's the Aerosol Kid from the Ghetto. He's peering at Ethnic – and finally recognizes him. He begins to move off, stops to take one more confirmatory look, then saunters away . . . gradually breaking into a trot.

117. EXT. STREET OUTSIDE FIRE STATION. DAY

A small queue stands at the bus stop. Suddenly the phone in the nearby kiosk begins to ring. The people in the queue exchange puzzled glances. The ringing continues. Finally, a woman goes to the kiosk.

118. INT. KIOSK. CONTINUOUS. DAY

The woman hauls herself in and picks up the receiver, tentatively.

WOMAN: (*into phone*) Hello? (*pause*) Oh. Right. (*She turns to the door to look at the people in the bus queue.*) Hang on. (*She pushes the door open.*)

119. EXT. KIOSK. CONTINUOUS. DAY

The woman calls to a man in the queue carrying a briefcase.

WOMAN: Excuse me. It's for you. The man with the briefcase, she said.

The man is bemused. Everyone turns to look at him. As the woman leaves the kiosk, he goes in.

120. INT. KIOSK CONTINUOUS. DAY
The Man picks up the receiver.
MAN: (*into phone, warily*) Mr Langley speaking ...

121. INT. FIRE STATION KITCHEN/MESS CONTINUOUS. DAY
*By the window, Malcolm – almost beside himself with
stifled hysterics – is holding the phone. With him are
Rambo and Josie. Malcolm promptly hands the phone
to Josie, and Rambo passes her a piece of paper.
Bayleaf is in the kitchen, preparing a stack of cheese
and onion rolls.*
JOSIE: (*reading from paper into phone*) Oh, hello, you
don't know me ... I live at no. 176, further up on
the other side of the road ... and I see you going
for the bus every day ... and I think you're
fantastic. My name's Gloria, No. 176 ... so if you
fancy a nice ...

Malcolm promptly depresses the buttons to
disconnect her – and almost keels over in hysterics.
With an indulgent shake of the head, Josie passes
the note back to Rambo.

122. EXT. STREET OUTSIDE FIRE STATION
CONTINUOUS. DAY
The man comes out of the kiosk, looking a little
flushed. The queue is looking at him. He smiles at them
. . . then starts walking across the road and back up the
street, with increasing – albeit nervous – excitement . . .

123. INT. TATE'S OFFICE FIRE STATION. DAY
Tate is speaking into the phone.
TATE: Right, sir.
He replaces the receiver and starts for the door.

124. INT. WATCHROOM. DAY
Sick Note is reading a magazine. Tate pops his head in at the door.

TATE: Sorry to disturb you before he's even got his hand on her frilly knickers ...
Sick Note tries to cover the magazine with a log book.
... but the Station Commander's due at 1200 hours, so look lively.

SICK NOTE: No problem, I'll break a leg.

TATE: Don't you bloody dare!
He exits.

125. INT. CORRIDOR FIRE STATION. DAY
Tate passes Charisma walking along.

TATE: Station Commander here 1200 hours, Charisma. Don't stand to attention with a cue in your hand, alright? He's funny like that.

CHARISMA: Did I tell you I've battled through to the final at the Club, sir?
But Tate has already gone.
...Beat the favourite. 103 against 22. Felt sorry for him really. Big mate of mine.

126. INT. MESS/KITCHEN. DAY
Malcolm is still trying to recover from the phone-kiosk wheeze. Josie is offering him a glass of water. Rambo is patting his back. (Bayleaf is in the kitchen preparing cheese and onion rolls.) Tate walks into the Mess.

TATE: Malcolm?

MALCOLM: Yes, guv ... we were just checking the ...

TATE: Commander Petrie arrives 1200 hours. I want everybody looking as near like firemen as possible without resort to cosmetic surgery.

MALCOLM: Right, guv.
He, Rambo and Josie wander out.
Tate strolls over to the hatch. He stands glancing

93

from the cheese and onion rolls to Bayleaf and back again, hopefully. Bayleaf understands.

BAYLEAF: It'll be stand easy in ten minutes, guv ... Less.

TATE: Just one.

BAYLEAF: You'll be getting *two* at stand easy!

TATE: I'll have finished it by then ...
Bayleaf resignedly hands him one of the rolls.

BAYLEAF: It buggers up my counting, guv ...

TATE: You'll go to heaven, lad. They have computers.

127. INT. KITCHEN/MESS. LATER
Blue Watch – with the exception of JOSIE *– are at stand easy. Drinking tea, eating cheese and onion rolls. All seated round the table. Tate is about to start on his two rolls when he looks around at everyone's faces ... suddenly aware that something's wrong ...*

TATE: Hang about ... there's someone adrift ...
Everyone looks round, puzzled. Abruptly, Malcolm realizes who.

MALCOLM: Oh, Testicles! I sent her to the bank, didn't I?

TATE: (*a suspicious beat*) You *sent* her?

MALCOLM: *You* gave permission, guv ...

TATE: You said she thought her pay was bottlenecked or something, and she was scared to ask me ... But if *you* sent her, it wasn't that at *all*, was it? It was a bleedin' wheeze!

HALLAM: (*accusingly to Malcolm*) Would you like to tell the Commander one of the inmates has escaped and gone trolling down the High Street?

TATE: Malcolm, no one leaves a Station unless on a shout or in a strait-jacket. I bend the rules for an emergency, not a bleedin' wheeze!

MALCOLM: Sorry, guv.

TATE: When are you going to grow up, Malcolm?

MALCOLM: It's wheezes that keep me *out* of a strait-jacket ... Stuck with this lot day and night. Keeps me compos mentis.

TATE: You want to bet?

HALLAM: I'm impressed.

OTHERS: (*enjoying Malcolm's discomfort*) Very nice ... Leading Hand an' all... No sense of responsibility ... playing fields of Eton ...

TATE: (*to Malcolm*) Tell me something. Has she got in her little pinkies what I *think* she's got in her little pinkies?

128. EXT. STREET. DAY
Josie is walking into a bank, carrying a fire extinguisher and an envelope.

129. INT. BANK CONTINUOUS. DAY
Josie goes to a counter . . . getting a few funny looks
from other customers on the way.
JOSIE: Morning.
TELLER: Morning.
She hands him the envelope. He looks at her, a
little warily and opens it. Sighs. His suspicions are
confirmed.
You're new there, are you?
JOSIE: Sorry?
TELLER: The Fire Station.
JOSIE: (*thrown*) Well . . . a few weeks.
The Teller reads aloud from the note.
TELLER: 'This is a hold up. Give us your money or I'll
squirt this up your trouser-leg!'
Customers stop and stare.
JOSIE: (*muttering*) Bastards . . .
TELLER: Tell 'em to think up some new ones, will
you?

130. INT. STATION OFFICER'S OFFICE. DAY
The Commander is seated at the desk, going through
logs and paper-work with Tate and Hallam, who are
standing on either side of him.
COMMANDER: Okay, Bill. (*closes files*) Wheel him in.
Hallam goes to the door, opens it.

131. INT. CORRIDOR OUTSIDE OFFICE CONTINUOUS.
DAY
Ethnic stands, straightening his tie, drying his hands
down his uniform. Hallam pops his head round.
HALLAM: Alright, Fireman Lewis.
ETHNIC: Sir.
He goes in.

132. INT. STATION OFFICER'S OFFICE. CONTINUOUS.
DAY
Ethnic marches in. Hallam closes the door behind him.

96

COMMANDER: Morning, lad.

ETHNIC: Morning, sir.

The Commander taps an official memorandum on the desk.

COMMANDER: From the panel. Confirming your date. You start as Leading Fireman, 'A' Division on Saturday the 28th. If the dirty sods give you a cup of tea your first morning, don't drink it, you'll never know what they've put in it. (*beat*) Yes, you will. (*resumes*) So, that's it, lad. Congratulations and good luck.

ETHNIC: Thank you, sir.

TATE: And the same from us, laddie.

ETHNIC: Thank you, sir.

TATE: And I never want to see you back here below the rank of Station Officer, alright?

ETHNIC: No problem. I mean, 'Right, sir'.

The Commander shakes his hand, then is about to sit down again, when –

133. EXT. STATION YARD. CONTINUOUS. DAY

From the Commander's P.O.V., we see Josie returning into the station yard with her fire extinguisher.

134. INT. STATION COMMANDER'S OFFICE.
CONTINUOUS DAY

The Commander watches Josie cross the yard.

COMMANDER: Has she been outside?

HALLAM: (*guiltily*) Um . . . not actually out . . . well, only . . . um . . .

COMMANDER: She been doing what I think she's been doing?

TATE: (*peering out of the window, even more guiltily*) Um . . . what exactly is she . . .

COMMANDER: Not the old fire extinguisher one . . . Jesus . . . I thought that went out with horse-drawn machines . . .

INT. REST ROOM. DAY

Bayleaf, Vaseline, Malcolm, Sick Note, Rambo,
Charisma and Josie are in a conspiratorial circle of
armchairs. Bayleaf is checking the calendar.

BAYLEAF: So, if there's one night owing to him, his
last night here'll be the 22nd, right? 'Stead of the
23rd. So the 22nd, it is. That's when we do it.

VASELINE: *I* won't!

BAYLEAF: We *all* are!

VASELINE: I'm not eating that kind of muck! I'll bring
sandwiches.

BAYLEAF: You'll bring sandwiches.

VASELINE: I'll bring bleedin' sandwiches.

BAYLEAF: You've had three wives and 300 fiancées –
and not one of them's ever so much as buttered
you a slice of bread.

VASELINE: I'll go hungry then.

BAYLEAF: S'alright, he'll eat it intravenously. (*to the others*) You'll pull his pants off, you two hold him down, I'll stuff all three courses up his ...
Ethnic enters. Bayleaf at once falls silent.
Everyone tries vainly to look innocent.
ETHNIC: What's going on, then? (*beat*) Planning stuffing my pillow with billiard balls?
VASELINE: Do you lot ever eat anything edible?
They all immediately turn and yell 'Belt up!'
Ethnic looks at them, uncomprehending.
BAYLEAF: (*gently, by way of explanation*) It's a surprise. Piss off out.

136. INT. JOSIE AND GERRY'S BEDROOM. DAY
Josie is dressed in casual clothes. She's putting on make-up at a dressing table mirror. Gerry is standing behind her. They're quietly, bitingly, nearing the epicentre of what'll soon be a shouting match.
GERRY: Why *him*?
JOSIE: 'Cos he's the bleedin' Mess manager, inn'e?
GERRY: Why *you* then?
JOSIE: 'Cos it's me that wants cheap groceries, innit? Me and *you*, you stupid berk!
GERRY: Yeah, alright, leave out the language, you're not in the fire station now.
A pause ... while she bites back a yell, and speaks quietly and painstakingly instead.
JOSIE: Because he's the Mess Manager, he has the Cash 'n Carry card, right? Official. If I go with him, I can get stuff for *us* on his card, right? *Un*official. It's a little flanker, innit? Saves us a few bob.
He watches her applying her make-up.
GERRY: 'S'funny, innit? You tell me nothing about what goes on there, these days. You used to talk about nothing else.
JOSIE: (*defensively*) These days you don't want to know.

99

GERRY: It's your day off.
She grabs her handbag and starts for the door.
JOSIE: S'why it has to be today, innit? When else
could we go shopping?
She exits.
CUT TO:

137. INT. HALLWAY JOSIE'S FLAT CONTINUOUS. DAY
*Josie makes her way from the bedroom towards the
front door, grabbing her coat as she goes. Gerry comes
out of the bedroom and leans against the jamb.*
GERRY: *We* could've gone out . . .
She stops, look at him, sighs wryly.
JOSIE: (*simply*) Where? (*There's no answer. She goes
back to him, kisses him on the cheek. There's no
response from Gerry. A pause.*) See you in a bit.
She starts again for the front door.
GERRY: The whole point of being a fireman's wife is
having my husband *home* four days at a time . . .
Josie turns, troubled.
JOSIE: What?
GERRY *goes back into the bedroom, slamming the door
behind him. Josie angrily opens the front door and
goes.*

138. EXT. SUBURBAN STREET. DAY
*A bus is driving along. It begins to slow down for a bus
stop some way ahead.*

139. INT. BUS (TRAVELLING) CONTINUOUS. DAY
*Bayleaf, in undress uniform and cap, gets up from his
seat and makes his way towards the doors. As he
passes, an elderly man, seated with his wife, offers him
some coins.*
ELDERLY MAN: Two to Tottenham Court Road,
please.
BAYLEAF: Try the conductor.
ELDERLY MAN: (*baffled*) Eh?
BAYLEAF: I'm an admiral in the Fleet Air Arm.

ELDERLY MAN: Oh . . . sorry, sir. I thought you . . .
Bayleaf continues to the doors and gets off.
ELDERLY MAN'S WIFE: You'd think admirals go by car.
ELDERLY MAN: (*a beat*) Cut backs.
ELDERLY MAN'S WIFE: Oh.

140. EXT. CASH 'N CARRY DISCOUNT WAREHOUSE. DAY
Josie is waiting. She sees Bayleaf walking towards her.
JOSIE: What've you come all dolled up for?
BAYLEAF: Helps your cover-story, dunnit? (*she grins*) Anyway, every shirt I've got needs ironing.
JOSIE: So do my husband's.
BAYLEAF: (*sensing her despondency*) Are you alright?
JOSIE: Haven't you come in your car?
BAYLEAF: Vaseline's borrowed it to do an errand for me. He'll bring it back here in time for loading up. Good morning.
JOSIE: Good morning.
They go in.

141. EXT. MRS WEBB'S HOUSE. DAY
Vaseline is unloading cans of paint from the boot of a car. Mrs Webb stands on the doorstep watching, worriedly.
MRS WEBB: Six litres of what?
VASELINE: Autumn Blossom . . . just to show he's thinking of you . . . And he'll be here tomorrow morning to . . .
MRS WEBB: It isn't Autumn Blossom now. That was when we changed it from Golden Aubergine after we'd gone off Sudden Sunset after we'd gone off Golden Aubergine.
VASELINE: Right. (*beat*) What is it now?
MRS WEBB: Tranquil Dawn.
VASELINE: I'll . . . um . . . I'll tell him. You don't need your garden doing, by any chance?

MRS WEBB: What colour?
VASELINE: Sorry?
MRS WEBB: Garden?
VASELINE: S'alright ... forget it ...
He starts reloading the cans of paint.

142. EXT. BAYLEAF'S CAR CONTINUOUS. DAY
As it drives through north London. On the skyline in the distance is Alexandra Palace.

143. INT. BAYLEAF'S CAR (TRAVELLING). DAY
The boot and back seat are piled high with the unwanted cans of paint and stacks of groceries from the Cash 'n Carry. Bayleaf is driving; Josie in the passenger seat.
JOSIE: Where now?
BAYLEAF: Finsbury park ... for Ethnic's stuff.
Josie looks at Alexandra Palace.
JOSIE: Is that what I think it is?
BAYLEAF: Don't tell the guv'nor – he thinks it's made of matchsticks.
JOSIE: Why is he so hung up about it? It en't even his patch.
BAYLEAF: Grieves him, Ally Pally. The biggest job the Brigade's had since ... I dunno, the blitz maybe ... and we went and lost it, didn't we?
JOSIE: It looks alright from here.
BAYLEAF: Now, yeah. Now it's tarted up. It was gutted. Twenty-five pumps bleedin' their hearts out.
JOSIE: Twenty-five and they couldn't save it!
BAYLEAF: It was a fifty-pumper, Ally Pally. Officially stipulated. It needed every one of them.
A pause.
JOSIE: Well, why did it only get twenty-five?
BAYLEAF: Ah!
JOSIE: What?
BAYLEAF: If there was fifty at Ally Pally, the rest of

London was up the spout. Couple of decent-sized jobs somewhere else ... they'd've just had to burn.

JOSIE: Jesus.

BAYLEAF: So ... Politics, innit? Couldn't let all London know it hadn't enough machines to look after itself, right? So, ring, ring, Home Office, ring, ring, Fire Brigade ... and you get the biggest cut back, cock-up and cover-up since the Fire of London. Politics.

A pause.

JOSIE: Makes you feel stupid, dunnit? (*pause*) Is that why he's rebuilding it in matchsticks?

BAYLEAF: It helps him to kid himself it never happened.

They drive on in silence.

144. EXT. ASIAN DELICATESSEN. FINSBURY PARK. DAY

The car drives up and parks. Bayleaf gets out.

BAYLEAF: You stay here. Any traffic warden nonsense, flash your I.D. card and tell them we're checking the dry-riser.

He goes into the delicatessen.

145. INT. ASIAN DELICATESSEN CONTINUOUS. DAY

An Asian woman is working behind the counter. The other customers are all Asian or West Indian.

BAYLEAF: Morning.

ASIAN WOMAN: We don't sell cigarettes ...

BAYLEAF: Fine. How about pumpkins?

ASIAN WOMAN: Pumpkins is okay.

BAYLEAF: (*referring to his list*) Right. I want a three-pound pumpkin for starters. Well, not for starters, 'cos we're having the saltfish for starters ...

ASIAN WOMAN: Sorry?

BAYLEAF: And then I want ...

146. INT. BAYLEAF'S FLAT. KITCHEN. DAY
*Bayleaf is checking his list against a stack of exotic
groceries on the kitchen table. Josie is wandering
around the room, taking it all in.*

BAYLEAF: . . . cream, tabasco, nutmeg, akee,
chicken, cornmeal, mangoes –

JOSIE: You keep it nice.

BAYLEAF: Eh? (*looks at her looking round*) Oh. yeah.
I had a belt round this morning. (*resumes*) Okra,
yams –

JOSIE: Do you want to talk about her?

BAYLEAF: (*a beat*) No.

JOSIE: Well, that's a good sign.

BAYLEAF: Sweet potatoes, fig leaves . . .

JOSIE: Did you tell the lads? About your wife?

BAYLEAF: Yeah.

JOSIE: What did they say?

BAYLEAF: Nothing. They were watching *Dynasty*. All
they did was turn the sound up. (*pause*) What's
your old man like?

JOSIE: I'd sooner not talk about him either. (*beat*)
That's probably a *bad* sign. (*beat*) Shall we have a
cup of tea?

BAYLEAF: I'll do it.

She starts towards the kettle.

JOSIE: S'alright.

*Bayleaf immediately leaves his groceries and beats
her to it to the kettle.*

BAYLEAF: I said *I'd* do it.

*She steps back, resignedly amused to this latest
example of refusal of help. He starts busying
himself with the kettle. She watches him . . . for a
long moment.*

147. INT. HALLWAY ETHNIC'S PARENTS' FLAT. DAY
*We see the letterbox opening – and through it is pushed
a bottle with a burning rag extended from it. It crashes*

to the floor and bursts into violent flame. It's followed
by another.
  Reverse shot to see Beatrice framed in her living
room doorway. She sees the flames and starts to
scream. Eldridge and Ethnic join her at the doorway.
Ethnic crashes his way past them.
ETHNIC: Get out, Ma! Out de back way! Dad, get her
  out!
BEATRICE: My rent book! In me coat pocket!
ETHNIC: *(pulling her back)* Leave it! Everything! Just
  get out!
  He pushes her back. Eldridge hauls her back
  inside the living room. Ethnic runs down the
  hallway, tears coats from the hallstand, hurls them
  on to the fire and starts stamping on them.

148. EXT. GHETTO FLATS. DAY
The Aerosol Kid, one of the Rastas and Whitey are
leaning against the wall across the street,
expressionlessly watching the smoke billowing out from
under Ethnic's door.
  The other Rasta is leaping his way down the outside
stairway from the flat, to join them.
  Two policemen stroll by.

149. EXT. GHETTO. DAY
Beatrice, tears streaming down her face, runs towards
the Community Hall.

150. INT. HALLWAY ETHNIC'S PARENTS' FLAT. DAY
Ethnic is pouring two saucepans of water on to the
(now less violently) burning coats. Eldridge rushes
from the living room with a bucket of water, grabs the
saucepans and returns. Ethnic hurls the water on to the
coats.
  The fire is under control. Ethnic stands panting, his
eyes wet with smoke and anger.

The hallway is blackened and scorched, the coats are ruined, smouldering, occasionally flickering into flame.

151. EXT. GHETTO FLATS. DAY
The Aerosol Kid, Whitey and two Rastas watch as Ethnic opens the front door and kicks the smoking mess out on to the balcony.
One of the policemen glances up.
1ST P.C: Aye, aye . . .
  His colleague looks at him, then follows his eyes.
2ND POLICEMAN: 'S'okay. It's only a domestic.
  They continue on their patrol.

152. INT. COMMUNITY HALL. DAY
Beatrice is seated at the trestle table, clutching a cup of tea. Seated around her are Rose, two middle-aged women and an elderly man.
  They sit in silent sympathy as Beatrice sits trembling in shock. Rose has her arm round her.
  At the back of the hall, others are playing dominoes.
A silence, then –
BEATRICE: Why firemen? Why firemen, Rose?
ROSE: Boys aroun here, a whole heap act crazy
  sometimes . . .
1ST WOMAN: A whole heap aroun de *world* act crazy
  these days. Go anywhere, all de same.
BEATRICE: Firemen ent policemen. Firemen don't
  give no one bad time. Jus' put out de fires. Save
  people. Is bobbylan dey hate.
  A pause.
2ND WOMAN: T'aint *all* hate policeman.
1ST WOMAN: T'aint *all* policeman give us bad time.
2ND WOMAN: Rest. If you're *youth* and you're lime in
  de street, you get bad time. They think they *all*
  bad.
ROSE: Policeman have his work to do.
2ND WOMAN: Youth have *none*. No work to do. You
  reason with me? Is one vicious thing.

BEATRICE: Maybe *my* boy hang aroun after this.
Maybe I tell him stop being fireman.
ROSE: No, Bea.
A pause.
BEATRICE: Why firemen? It don't make sense.
A pause.
ROSE: Not one piece of it make sense.
OLD MAN: Cha! Of course it does! (*they look at him, shocked*) You stick a bunch of rats in a cage, good rats, bad rats, they got nothin to eat, what gonna happen den? They go crazy, they eat each *other*. Them that ain't so crazy get their flesh chewed off first. White rats, black rats, all de same. (*beat*) All de same underneath. Same white bones picked clean. (*beat*) Either you open de cage, or you throw in more cheese. (*beat*) Or maybe . . .they

chew through de bars with their sharp white
teeth. And what den?
Hold for a long, bleak moment, then –

153. INT. RECREATION ROOM FIRE STATION. DAY
*Charisma is playing snooker on his own. Apart from
his one spectator – Josie – the room is deserted.
Charisma plays a shot.*
CHARISMA: That's positional play, you see. Cue ball
up behind the green, giving me a chance for the
next red.
JOSIE: *(mystified)* Right.
CHARISMA: Mind you, it's a doddle in here. The Club
tournament final – that's a different ball-game.
JOSIE: *(baffled)* Not snooker?
CHARISMA: Yeah.
JOSIE: *(more baffled)* Oh. Right.
CHARISMA: I mean that's *pressure*, innit? That's your
test of character for your big-match temperament.
'Course, most of 'em's my mates.
JOSIE: Right.
CHARISMA: All rooting for me. You know, with it
being the big one.
JOSIE: Who's going from here?
CHARISMA: Going where?
JOSIE: To watch you.
CHARISMA: *(a beat)* I didn't invite 'em, 'cos of prior
engagements. I doubt they'd get in, anyway, once
my Fan Club's turned up . . .
*Josie watches him playing. The look of pity on her
face changes to one of pensiveness – then of
decision. Rambo pops his head in at the door.*
RAMBO: Firewoman Ingham, please.
JOSIE: Oh, hell, as formal as that, is it?
RAMBO: I'm not at liberty to enter into discussions.
Follow me.
JOSIE: Oh. Right.

154. INT. CORRIDOR FIRE STATION CONTINUOUS. DAY
Rambo leading Josie down the corridor.
JOSIE: Will I have to stand to attention or can I swing
from a lightbulb?
RAMBO: Remain silent, please.
JOSIE: Did you know half your bum's lopsided?
He leads her into the Mess.

155. INT. MESS/KITCHEN CONTINUOUS. DAY
*Seated around the table – as though at an emergency
Cabinet Meeting – are Malcolm, Bayleaf, Ethnic,
Vaseline and Sick Note. It's nearing the end of the
lunch hour. Some of them are still eating. Malcolm has
a small pile of pieces of paper in front of him.*
Rambo leads Josie in.
RAMBO: Firewoman Ingham.
SICK NOTE: I knew I recognized the face.
Bayleaf cuffs him. Rambo sits down.
JOSIE: Well?
MALCOLM: We haven't decided.
JOSIE: What??
BAYLEAF: Not unanimously.
JOSIE: I've been sat out there half an hour!
MALCOLM: Everyone's got a different one. No one'll
give way.
JOSIE: What are they? *I'll* pick one.
VASELINE: Well, that's no good, is it? You'll pick one
you *like*. Defeats the purpose.
*Malcolm sifts through the scraps of paper, one by
one, reading a scribbled nickname from each.*
MALCOLM: By the authority vested in me as
Returning Officer for Blue Watch ...
SICK NOTE: Jesus ...
MALCOLM: ... the results of the secret ballot held in
the above constituency ...
BAYLEAF: Just read them, Malcolm.
MALCOLM: ... for the nickname of Firewoman
Ingham are as follows ...

Josie pretends an enormous yawn. Malcolm looks at her, irritatedly.

JOSIE: (*innocently*) Oh, sorry, are you ready?

MALCOLM: (*first paper*) 'Soul Sister' ...(*second paper*) 'Mother Superior' ... (*third paper*) 'Kicker' ...

JOSIE: 'Kicker'?

MALCOLM: (*peers at paper*) As in 'I wouldn't kick her out of bed'.

JOSIE: Nice. So far I'm a sister, a mother, a nun and a tart ...

MALCOLM: (*fourth paper*) Affro ...

Josie glances at Ethnic.

ETHNIC: Not me.

MALCOLM: (*peering at paper*) As in Aphrodisiac. (*fifth paper*) 'Janet Reger'.

JOSIE: Janet Reger?

MALCOLM: They make knickers. It's a knicker-name. Compris? Nickname – knickername. (*He titters. Everyone else groans.*) And 'Wozzo'. As in, 'She was only a fireman's daughter ...'

JOSIE: (*looks at each of them, wryly*) A sister, a mother, a daughter, a nun, a tart, Spanish Fly and a pair of knickers ...

BAYLEAF: Tells us a lot about you, dunnit?

JOSIE: (*slow smile*) Um ... no, not about *me*, lads.

156. A TV SCREEN
rapidly changing from a commercial – to a Western – to an opera ...

157. INT. BAYLEAF'S FLAT. NIGHT
Bayleaf is sprawled in an easy chair, pressing the channel changes on his TV remote control. He has a can of beer and a plate of half-eaten sandwiches. He flicks through the programmes again, and finally lands on a snooker tournament between, say, Steve Davis and Cliff Thorburn.
*   He watches for a few moments ... and a worrying*

*thought slowly dawns on him. He suddenly jerks a look
at his watch.*

BAYLEAF: Oh, shit!!
*He leaps to his feet, races to his phone at the other
side of the room and starts to dial, agitatedly.*

158. INT. JOSIE'S/GERRY'S HALLWAY CONTINUOUS.
NIGHT
*The phone stands ringing in the half-lit room. The flat's
deserted.*

159. INT. BAYLEAF'S HALLWAY CONTINUOUS. NIGHT
*Bayleaf races in from the living room, grabs his coat
and races out of the front door.*

160. INT. WORKING MEN'S CLUB. NIGHT
*A bar, a small stage, a few fruit machines and a billiard
table. Two men are playing snooker, a third is acting as
referee (with a pint of beer in his hand).*
   *A smallish crowd of members and their wives are
seated around the table, watching the match.*
*One of the players pots the black. The referee picks it
out of the pocket, and replaces it on its spot.*
REFEREE: Eight.
   *At the door, a Club official admits Josie and
   Gerry. A whispered conversation. Josie hands him
   a pound. He gestures that they go in.*
   Josie turns and stares at the two players. Puzzled.
   She turns to a man standing next to her.
JOSIE: When's the final?
MAN: Now.
JOSIE: (*bewildered*) This??
MAN: Harry's winning one frame to nil.
JOSIE: Isn't . . . isn't Mr Appleby in it?
MAN: Who's Mr Appleby?
   The player misses the ball.
REFEREE: Harry – 22.

Josie stares at the marker adding 22 to the
scoreboard. It's Charisma.

JOSIE: Um . . . *he* is.

MAN: Don't know him. Seen him around, I think.
He's the marker.

JOSIE: And isn't he in it?

MAN: (*beat*) Yeah. The bleedin' marker!
The next player goes in-off. The referee calls.

REFEREE: Foul stroke. Four to Harry.
Charisma adds it to the scoreboard.
Josie looks devastated. Gerry sighs impatiently.

161. EXT. WORKING MEN'S CLUB. NIGHT
Josie and Gerry come out and start walking to the car
park.

GERRY: Good, that. Only cost us a quid. Good job
we're flush.

JOSIE: Poor Charisma ... poor sod ...
A car pulls into a space ahead. Bayleaf gets out.
As he's locking the door, Josie and Gerry walk by.
Josie and Bayleaf see each other. Gerry looks from
one to another.
JOSIE: (*pleased, surprised*) Hi.
BAYLEAF: Good. Caught you.
JOSIE: Don't go in. He en't even *in* the final.
BAYLEAF: 'Course not.
JOSIE: All these big mates. No one's even ...
BAYLEAF: 'Course not. That's why I came ... in case
you did. Don't tell the lads. Don't even tell *him*.
(*to Gerry*) How de do.
JOSIE: Oh, sorry ... this is Gerry ... this is Bayleaf.
Bayleaf – Gerry.
BAYLEAF: (*offers his hand*) The real name's Mike.
GERRY: (*ignoring his hand*) Yeah? I think mine's
Wally, innit?
He smiles coldly. Bayleaf and Josie glance at each
other.

162. INT. TATE'S LIVING ROOM. DAY
Nancy is pouring tea for the wives of Vaseline, Rambo,
Hallam, Malcolm and Sick Note; and Charlene.
The coffee table is set with cakes and biscuits.
There's an uncomfortable silence. Everybody avoids
everybody else's eyes ... giving the most fractional of
tight smiles if their glances actually meet.
After a few moments, the doorbell rings.
NANCY: (*puzzled*) We're all here, aren't we? No stray
wife or girlfriend still to come ...?
Everyone looks blank.
MARION II: Unless it's some of my old feller's exes.
The doorbell rings again.
NANCY: 'Scuse me.
She makes for the door.

163. EXT. TATE'S HOUSE. DAY
Gerry is on the doorstep – dressed at his smartest.
Nancy opens the door.
GERRY: Mrs Tate.
NANCY: Yes?
GERRY: Gerry Ingham. I've come for the orgy.
NANCY: Pardon?

164. INT. TATE'S LIVING ROOM. DAY
Nancy is introducing Gerry to the ladies.
NANCY: Betty Cross, Jean Quigley, Marion
    Cartwright, Carol Baines, Sandra Hallam and
    Charlene. And this is Gerry. (*He grins. They all
    stare at him blankly.*) . . . The first time we've had
    a man at our afternoon teas, really. Gerry is
    Firewoman Ingham's husband . . . Um, sit down,
    Gerry. (*He sits.*) Tea?
GERRY: Ta.
    Nancy starts to pour.
GERRY: You have these a lot, do you?
NANCY: Oh . . . a couple of times a year . . . It's my
    husband's idea . . . just a little social . . .
GERRY: Yeah, the missus said I should come . . . For a
    laugh. I mean she *said* it for a laugh . . .
    A silence. He looks at them one by one.
    Not funny, though, is it? You can't stand the sight
    of each other.
    A shocked frisson among the ladies.
NANCY: Sorry?
GERRY: Rumour has it. Why should you? Just 'cos
    your husbands are firemen doesn't mean you've
    anything *else* in common. (*pause*) Apart from
    wondering what they're up to half the time.
    (*He's hit right where it hurts. A prickly silence.*)
    Hard not to when they're sleeping out two nights
    a week. (*grins*) The way I see it, though, if they
    have two nights away from you . . . how do *they*
    know what *you're* up to . . . (*He turns to Jean*

Quigley. Smiles hard and long at her.) . . . Joan, is
it?

JEAN: (*shyly, heart leaping*) Jean.

GERRY: You follow my meaning, Jean?

*They smile into each other's eyes. The others look
shocked . . . then slowly more and more
intrigued . . .*

165. INT. RECREATION ROOM. NIGHT
*A cheap (but ornate) snooker trophy stands on the
snooker table. Vaseline is rummaging in a box which
he's dragged out of a locker.*

CHARISMA: He took it like a man, mind you. I mean,
you can't argue with a break of 86, can you? I was
a bit lucky on the double on the brown . . .

VASELINE: (*still rummaging*) Why dunnit say your
name?

CHARISMA: How d'you mean?

VASELINE: On your Capo de Monte?

CHARISMA: It's not Capo de Monte. It's the official
trophy of the –

VASELINE: Why dunnit say your name?

CHARISMA: I've to send it back to be engraved.

VASELINE: Oh.

*He finds what he's searching for. A clothes peg.
He puts it on his nose, and shoves the box back in
the locker.*

CHARISMA: At the engraver's . . .

Vaseline starts to exit, peg on nose.

I knew you'd all want to see it, that's all . . .

But Vaseline has now gone.

166. INT. COMMUNITY HALL GHETTO. EVENING
*Ethnic, Claude, Maxwell and Lloyd are rehearsing a
Ghetto Blaster number. This time they're playing their
kind of music – and having a great time. A few older
folk, playing dominoes at the other end of the hall,
aren't enjoying it quite so much, as their sighing and*

wincing indicates. This makes it even more *fun to Ethnic and his pals.*

167. EXT. GHETTO CONTINUOUS EVENING
As the Ghetto Blaster's music continues over, we see the Pusher leaning aimlessly against a wall, hands in pockets. With sudden-wary eyes, he watches two policemen strolling towards him. He tenses.
The policemen pass by. He relaxes again – and watches them continue towards the young men messing about with their old banger. The policemen stand one of the young men against the car and start to search him. A small gathering of passers-by begins to form and (at first, mildly) remonstrate with the policemen on behalf of the innocent young man. As the crowd grows bigger – and angrier – the Pusher gently levers himself off the wall and nonchalantly makes his way through them, and away from the trouble.

168. INT. KITCHEN/MESS CONTINUOUS. NIGHT
In the kitchen, the ingredients for the West Indian meal are ranged out on the table. Pans are bubbling on the stove, the oven is lit. Bayleaf is painstakingly cooking . . . following a recipe written on a sheet of paper.
At the hatch, Josie is writing out an elaborate menu in a thick, felt-tipped pen: 'Starters . . . Akee, saltfish, and fried plantains. Soup: . . . Cream of Pumpkin. Entree: . . . Coo-coo with Ashanti Chicken, yams and sweet potatoes. Dessert: . . . Pamie in fig-leaves . . . mango-ade (non-alcoholic)'.
Vaseline walks in with the clothes peg on his nose.
VASELINE: 'Scuse me, Witchdoctor.
BAYLEAF: (*too busy to look at him*) Hoppit.
VASELINE: All that's for *tomorrow* night, right?
JOSIE: Right.
VASELINE: Well, what the hell are we having *tonight*?
Bayleaf swivels round, horrified. He looks at

*Josie: He'd completely forgotten. She's equally
horrified.*

BAYLEAF: Oh, hell.

VASELINE: Exactly. (*taps his watch*) Ten past eight.

BAYLEAF: (*to Josie, urgently*) What's quick?

VASELINE: There's grown men out there, chewing
hosepipes . . .

BAYLEAF: (*to Josie*) Think!

JOSIE: My head won't work . . .

VASELINE: Guvnor'll be alright, of course. HP
sandwiches . . .

JOSIE: (*to Bayleaf*) How about egg and chips?

BAYLEAF: (*to Vaseline*) How about egg and chips?

VASELINE: (*disgusted*) Terrific. *He* turns up tomorrow
for a golliwog bleedin' *banquet*. He gets a night
off – and *we* get egg and chips!

*He wanders out. Josie leaps to her feet. Starts for
the kitchen.*

JOSIE: I'll do it!
BAYLEAF: Thanks.
She stops dead. Can't believe her ears.
JOSIE: (*small smile*) You don't mind?
BAYLEAF: Well, come on if you're coming! (*Her smile broadens. She continues into the kitchen. Bayleaf avoids her smile – and the end of an era.*) Spuds in there. Eggs in the fridge. Give 'em plenty of bread ...
As they race into action ...

169. INT. KITCHEN ETHNIC'S PARENTS' FLAT. NIGHT
Open on Beatrice dishing up eggs and chips from frying pans on to plates.

170. INT. ETHNIC'S PARENTS' LIVING ROOM CONTINUOUS. DAY
Charlene is sewing the Leading Fireman insignia on to Ethnic's uniform. Eldridge is reading the paper. Ethnic is snoozing.
BEATRICE (O.O.V.): Okay. All ready. (*She enters with plates of eggs and chips. Sees the table set for the meal. She's delighted.*) Hey! You set the table, Eldridge!
ELDRIDGE: No ... Charlene did it.
BEATRICE: Charlene's a visitor!
CHARLENE: That's all right, Mrs Lewis. Mr Lewis say he was readin' the cricket.
BEATRICE: He *always* say he readin' the cricket. Twenty-five years, every tea-time, he's readin' the cricket ...
ETHNIC *wakes up. Watches them for a moment.*
ETHNIC: Ssshh!
Everyone stops.
BEATRICE: What's wrong?
ETHNIC: Listen.
Everyone listens.

ELDRIDGE: I can't hear nothin.
ETHNIC: 'S'what I mean.

171. EXT. GHETTO. NIGHT
*Various shots of streets. All silent and deserted. The
only signs of life are pairs of patrolling policemen and
perhaps a stray dog or two . . . All aware of the eerie,
apprehensive silence . . .*

*Suddenly, we hear a stick tapping on a dustbin. Then
another and another. The police look first towards one
source of tapping, then another, then to another.
Swiftly beating an orchestrated tattoo like drums.*

*Shadowy figures flit from door to door, then
disappear.*

*Then, abruptly, the old banger we've previously
seen, bursts into flames. Police blow whistles. Just as
abruptly, another car bursts into flames.*

Police begin to run down the street towards the burning cars. As they reach them, a hail of bricks and stones showers down on them, seemingly from nowhere.

172. INT. FIRE BRIGADE CONTROL CENTRE CROYDON. NIGHT
The room is electric with activity. Officers, operators all working at top speed. All the VDU screens are flashing ... scores of calls, almost all of them reporting the riot.
OPERATOR: (*to Nancy*) Again. P22 Station J26 B25 PL and P. (*Nancy types it out on her computer.*) Your Sid's lot now ...
NANCY: All London, nearly ... everybody ...
CLOSE ON VDU *as she types ... 'Civil disturbance. Repeat. Civil disturbance. 44 P.2. 85. B25 PLP. All appliances.*

173. EXT. GHETTO. NIGHT
*The riot is at its peak. Shouts, screams, chants, the
frightening rhythmic metallic banging, crashing
masonry, police whistles, police sirens, the clanging of
fire-appliance bells.*
INSERT – *hands bolting the insides of doors in the flats.
Doors and windows being barricaded.
Outside, mobs of black and white youths hurl
missiles at serried ranks of riot-shielded, riot-helmeted
police.*
   *Injured policemen reel back. Injured blacks try to
escape.
Police cars and transport vehicles block off streets.
Several fire appliances and scores of firemen battle with
blazing cars, rubbish dumps and buildings. Among
them is Blue Watch. They're all under attack from the
rioters . . . from hurled missiles and from mob attacks
on individual firemen with sticks and crowbars.*
   *Ambulances race to the ear-splitting, terrifying,
jagged chaos.*
   *Another missile is flung from a balcony down on to
the police. It's the Pusher's TV set.*

174. INT. FIRE STATION. NIGHT
Each room silent and deserted.
   *The station cat pads along the corridor to the open
door of Tate's office. It goes in.*
   We hear a sudden crash.

175. INT. TATE'S OFFICE. NIGHT
*The cat is on his desk. The matchstick model of Ally
Pally lies in pieces on the floor.*

176. INT. FIRE BRIGADE CONTROL CENTRE. NIGHT
*The scene is as frenzied as before. Suddenly we hear a
voice from the scene of the riot over the radio speaker
. . . together with its background cacophony of screams,
shouts and crashing.*

VOICE: Impossible ... Can't get to ... Look out, lads!
Get back! Sod the fire! ... No access to ... We
can't ... We're in ... We're under attack ...
We're under attack ...
*Everyone listens, tensely. Nancy is white. She takes
another call.*

177. EXT. GHETTO. NIGHT
*Peeping fearfully through the curtains we see the faces
of residents. In one of them, the old man from the
Community Centre, mouthing a prayer.*
*Ethnic stands at his front door watching the violence
around him ... shaking his head, almost in tears.*
   *Further along the balcony, a gang of youths stands
piling up paving stones and missiles. The din is
terrifying. A scream pierces it. Ethnic turns towards it.
From Ethnic's P.O.V. in the street, we see a black*

youth pinned against a wall, being attacked by two
policemen.

   Ethnic watches a moment longer, then races along
the balcony past the youths with the paving-stones.
Leaps down the staircase, six steps at a time, and runs
into the street.

   He hears another cry.

   He stops.

   From his P.O.V., we see Charisma being attacked by
three youths with knives, hammers and sticks.

   Ethnic looks from one group to another.

   The black youth cries again for help.

   Charisma screams for help.

   INTERCUT *between the two of them – and Ethnic . . .*
torn between the two, faced with an impossible
dilemma.

   Sobbing and moaning in anger and hopelessness, he

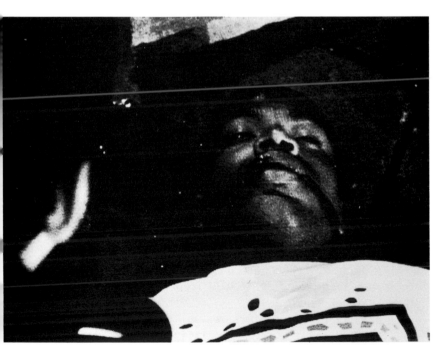

suddenly turns and races to Charisma's aid. He crashes through the attackers and drags him clear of them. As more police rush up, Charisma's attackers race away from the scene.

Ethnic turns to see the black youth still cornered by the policemen.

CUT TO

the youths on the balcony. They heave a paving-stone on to the balustrade – and push it over the edge.

CUT TO

Ethnic – as the paving-stone crashes down on his head.

CUT TO

Charisma as he scrambles to his feet and goes over to Ethnic's prostrate body.

He kneels over him, turns him gently over to see his face. It's covered in blood.

Ethnic looks at him, unseeingly, for a moment, then his eyes start to close. Blood trickles from his mouth. A spasm . . . and he dies.

DISSOLVE TO:

178. EXT. GHETTO IN L.S. DAWN
Burnt-out cars and buildings, wreckage, debris: emptiness and silence as dawn breaks. A ghost town.

179. INT. TATE'S OFFICE. EARLY MORNING
TATE *sits slumped in his chair, his face blackened, his uniform torn.*

There's a knock at the door. He doesn't react.

The door opens, and Josie enters carrying a mug of tea. He still sits motionless.

She puts the mug down on the desk. Then sees the wrecked model of Ally Pally on the floor.

She picks it up and puts it on the desk. Tate ignores it. She takes a match from the box and puts it between his fingers, for him to start modelling.

124

He looks at her. She nods solemnly. He shakes his head.

TATE: What for?

JOSIE: Fun.

180. EXT. GHETTO. DAY
A policeman stands guard over the outlined shape of Ethnic's body where he died, chalked on the ground.
    The Street Kid from Scene 1 sits watching, playing with a piece of glass.
PAN UP TO
the front door of Ethnic's parents' flat. On it is a black wreath.

181. INT. ETHNIC'S PARENTS' FLAT. DAY
Beatrice, Eldridge, Charlene, a priest and Lloyd sit in silence.

Beatrice is holding Ethnic's uniform jacket with the new insignia sewn on.
It slips from her fingers to the floor. Lloyd leans forward, puts it back in her hands, and closes her hands securely over it.

182. INT. STATION MESS/KITCHEN. NIGHT
Tate, Hallam, Malcolm, Josie, Vaseline, Rambo, Charisma and Sick Note are seated at the table, their West Indian meal in front of them.
Bayleaf comes from the kitchen carrying his own plate. He sits at the table. Everyone starts to eat in silence.
Josie gives Bayleaf a small, sad smile – indicating it's good. A small, sad, smile back. After a few moments, Charisma pushes his plate gently away, his eyes filled with tears.
Vaseline pushes it gently back in front of him again.

*Charisma looks at him and shakes his head. Vaseline's
eyes stay fixed on him. Charisma starts eating again . . .*
SLOW DISSOLVE TO:

183. INT/EXT. APPLIANCE ROOM. DAY
*Some months later. Blue Watch stand in line facing
Tate and Hallam. Lloyd is now a fireman.*
TATE: *(in* C.U.) Call the roll.
HALLAM: *(in* C.U.) Blue Watch – attention! Answer
    your names. Leading Fireman Cross.
MALCOLM: *(in* C.U.) Yes, sir.
Bayleaf – in C.U.
HALLAM (O.O.S.): Fireman Wilson.
BAYLEAF: Sir.
Josie – in C.U.
HALLAM (O.O.S.): Firewoman Ingham.

JOSIE: Sir.

Vaseline – in C.U.

HALLAM (O.O.S.): Fireman Cartwright.

VASELINE: Sir.

Charisma – in C.U.

HALLAM (O.O.S.): Fireman Appleby.

CHARISMA: Sir.

Rambo – in C.U.

HALLAM (O.O.S.): Fireman Baines.

RAMBO: Sir.

Sick Note – in C.U.

HALLAM (O.O.S.): Fireman Quigley.

SICK NOTE: Sir.

Lloyd – in C.U.

HALLAM (O.O.S.): Fireman Anderson.

LLOYD: Sir.

HALLAM (O.O.S.): Welcome to Blue Watch.

LLOYD: Thank you, sir.

HALLAM: Blue Watch, stand at ease!

WIDE SHOT, CRANING FURTHER AND FURTHER BACK
The sound of Hallam's voice gradually fades as he continues . . .

HALLAM: Riders for appliances are as follows: On the pump ladder, myself, Fireman Appleby driving. Plus Leading Fireman Cross and Fireman Baines. On the pump, Station Officer Tate, Fireman Wilson driving. Plus Fireman Anderson, Fireman Quigley and Firewoman Ingham. Watchroom – Fireman Cartwright.
Detached Duty-Fireman Rippon; Fireman Henderson, acting up. Fireman Grey – Long term sick. Chemical Protection Suits Anderson and Ingham, Baines and Cross.
Blue Watch attention! For duty – fall out.
They all move to the machines and start checking the equipment. During the above, credits begin to roll.